MIRIAM JOY'S
WAX DESIGN TECHNIQUE

FOR GOURDS, WOOD & CRAFTS

Schiffer
Publishing Ltd

4880 Lower Valley Road • Atglen, PA 19310

To the memory of my Grandmother....

When I see flowers, I always go back to her immaculate flower garden, with kids by her side, letting us pick them to put together arrangements of bright colors and sweet smells. She taught me how to make beautiful things using ordinary items, nature, and lots of imagination — proving time and time again that if you can dream it, you can make it happen. May memories of her in her flower garden always linger in my heart. Grandmother, this book is dedicated to you...I am dreaming big!

Other Schiffer Books on Related Subjects:
Antler Art for Baskets and Gourds, 978-0-7643-3615-7, $19.99
Coiled Designs for Gourd Art, 978-0-7643-3011-7, $14.99
InLace Techniques: Resin Inlay for Gourd and Wood Crafts, 978-0-7643-3330-9, $12.99
New and Different Materials for Weaving and Coiling, 978-0-7643-3992-9, $29.99

Designed by Danielle D. Farmer
Type set in Alhambra/Cicero Caps/Calibri

ISBN: 978-0-7643-4467-1
Printed in the United States of America

Published by Schiffer Publishing, Ltd.
4880 Lower Valley Road
Atglen, PA 19310
Phone: (610) 593-1777; Fax: (610) 593-2002
E-mail: Info@schifferbooks.com

For our complete selection of fine books on this and related ⟨   ⟩te for a free catalog.

This book may be purchased from the publisher. Please try your bookstore first.

We are always looking for people to write books on new and related subjects. If you have an idea for a book, please contact us at **proposals@schifferbooks.com**

Schiffer Publishing's titles are available at special discounts for bulk purchases for sales promotions or premiums. Special editions, including personalized covers, corporate imprints, and excerpts can be created in large quantities for special needs. For more information, contact the publisher.

ACKNOWLEDGMENTS

I would love to thank the Lord for allowing me to use the talent that he has given me on loan. He has created all the wonderful things around us that inspire me deeply. I could not do any of this without his blessings.

To my wonderful and loving husband, Bud: You are always by my side. You are my biggest fan. I know that you always have my back. You believe in me 100%. Because of you, I am stronger, more caring, and loving my life. You give me wings to fly and, if I should fall, you would catch me. My life has changed so much since I met you...all for the better. You are my best friend and truly my soulmate. Thank you for being my manager, driver, supply person, and salesman. I love you.

To all the people who have helped make "Miriam Joy" a success: From the family who is always there with support and prayers to all the wonderful friends, thank you for all your help with our business and, most of all, for being just wonderful people. May I always be blessed with great people in our lives.

To my children: You believed in me and have helped me with so much. Your love and support has helped me become who I am in so many ways.

To all of my Navajo friends and family: Thank you for all the great talent that you shared. Thank you for showing me the beauty of the world around us, the red of the mountains, the blue of the skies, the white of the puffy clouds, and all the wonderful colors of the sunset. You taught me to see Mother Earth and all of her beauty in a different way.

To all the wonderful people I have met along the way, those who have opened their homes and hearts to me: I thank God for each and every one of you.

ADDING A LITTLE
"JOY"
TO YOUR LIFE.

CONTENTS

FOREWORD

ECCLESIASTES 1:9

"What has been will be again, / what has been done will be done again; / there is nothing new under the sun."

In a traditional hobby such as gourd crafting, it is seems fitting that there are so many "brown" gourds — gourds decorated with rich earth tones, reflective of the nature of something grown from the earth. Imagine then, my surprise a few years ago when Miriam Joy and her husband Bud came to one of our local gourd club meetings with unusually decorated gourds, filled with bold wax colors.

I have to admit I was a bit skeptical at first. Years ago, the hot Arizona climate had prompted some harsh words from me and a few tears from my children when their crayons melted all over the carpet in the back of the family station wagon! Despite this memory, I was intrigued with what I saw.

The next thought that struck me was great pleasure in seeing how this new artist had come up with an innovative and creative way to decorate her gourds. It was obvious that many hours had been spent perfecting her technique: discovering the best raw materials, the most functional tools, and coming up with interesting designs and patterns. Her gourds were eye-catching, and her enthusiasm for her technique was contagious.

As an artist myself, I realize how easy it is to just go with the flow and do what everyone else is doing. When you see something new and different, your first thought might be "Why didn't I think of that?" In the gourd crafting community, there is a generous spirit of sharing. Nothing stays new for too long - but certain techniques or styles become an artists' signature style. I doubt many people will look at wax embellished gourds without thinking of Miriam Joy.

With her warm and generous spirit, Miriam Joy shares her ideas and skills with you in the following chapters. Enjoy the process and have fun experimenting!

BONNIE GIBSON,
Arizona Gourds

INTRODUCTION

The wax process came about from my love of trying new things. I have always been a type of craft chemist. If I had not tested things people told me would not work, I would not be doing the art I am today. Never let anyone tell you something will not work. Try it and see if it turns into something wonderful. If not, then you know for sure. Test your limits.

I was introduced to gourd art a few years ago. Being a tole painting teacher, it seemed like another type of wood to paint. I have always loved texture and bright colors. I found an old low-temp melting pot in my craft room and thought, what can I do with this? God laid it on my heart to try melting crayons in it, which I had to then figure out how to apply onto a gourd. I had a few crude tools that I used in the beginning. I knew I wanted to do more with this technique. My husband was a big influence. He asked me to do a tree with the "wax stuff that I had been messing with" for our church auction. I told him it would never work. Did I say never say never? Dozens of trees later, here we are. I asked people to make me some crude tools because I knew that I wanted to do more things with the bright color wax that I had started applying to gourds. The wax worked well with the gourds. The gourds are porous and the wax attached itself to them — unlike everyone's fear that the wax would just pop off. I had people advise me to start teaching this technique. When I started to teach classes, I realized that I needed to sell a product line of tools I created so that people could go home and make more beautiful gourds. This is how my dream and goals became a reality.

The process is colorful and simple to learn, and it is so visually rewarding. The texture is puffy and gives it a great look. Pictures do not do it justice. Gourd artists of any level will love the process. It can be done in less than an hour up to as long and as detailed as you want to make it. The wax can also be combined with other techniques to give it a fresh look and nice texture. Once you learn the technique, you can add your own twist. Think of all the things you love and how you can use the Crayola Crayons® to create that. Be inspired by a pattern, a shirt, or a purse. You will start to see all kinds of patterns everywhere you look. Your imagination will know no limits.

Come and learn with me. Let me pour into you the knowledge that I have learned. My wish for you is that you enjoy it as much as I do. Let me add a little "Joy" to your life!

WARNINGS AND PRECAUTIONS

1. Low Temp Melting Pot, Wax Design Tools, and the Texture Brush and Insert can all get very **HOT.** Use caution and do not touch the hot metal when using or handling these items.

2. Always have **adult** supervision in cases where children are using the Wax Design. Safety allows fun for everyone! Wax Design is not recommended for children under eight years of age.

3. The melting pot is an electrical device —caution should be used while using any electrical device.

4. Use caution when working with a hobby knife: If the tool can cut through a crayon, that means it's sharp!

5. Unplug the melting pot when not in use.

Supplies used in Wax Design

USING AND MELTING CRAYOLA CRAYONS®

The wax that I use to decorate my gourds with is Crayola Crayons. Other crayons are too thin and the color is not as bright. Crayola is the superior product and has the best color pigment. Other waxes, such as bee's wax, are very thin and you have to add color to them. The cost is also a factor. When you get a box of Crayola Crayons, you now have all of these bright and wonderful colors all in one box and for a great price. Most of the gourds I create are done with less than one crayon, so it is very cost-effective. Think of what you could do with a box of 120 crayons!

Box of 24 Crayons

Each color goes on a little different. REALLY! The lighter colors, like yellow and the yellow-greens, are thinner. It is not anything you are doing wrong. The dark colors are thicker and drip less. However, the white thinks it is a dark color, as it has a lot of pigment.

When you are looking at your crayon, look at the tip of the crayon. This is the color your wax will be -- not the color of the wrapper. The dark purples and blues will almost be black. When working with the dark colors, I add a little bit of white crayon to lighten them up closer to the color of the wrapper.

Treat your crayons just like paints. You can mix and match your crayons to make different colors or make lighter and darker shades. I use the blue-green and white mixed 50/50 to make my turquoise color. The box of twenty-four Crayola Crayons is the most cost-effective and the easiest to find. It has a great range of colors for my pallet. I teach and create most of my gourds and artwork using these twenty-four colors, as well as mixing them. Keeping track of the amounts you mix and the

Crayola Crayons

colors you use enables you to mix more of the same color. The box of twenty-four Crayola Crayons goes on sale during the "Back to School" season, with the price discounted by fifty to seventy-five percent, making it a great time to stock up for the year.

Metallic Crayons

The bigger boxes have more of a variety of crayons. There are the metallic crayons, which are a big hit with everyone. Fun colors like gold, silver, and bronze are among the favorites. You can also find a box of Crayola Metallic FX Crayons® in a pack of sixteen wonderful colors. While these are a little harder to find, look for them in the Crayola section of stores or you can order them from my website, www.miriamjoy.com. Metallic crayons are great accent colors and wonderful to use for Christmas ornaments or other fun holiday projects. When melted into wax, these colors are a little thinner than regular crayons and need to be stirred a little more, but the effect is wonderful. They add shine and glow to your artwork.

The bigger boxes of Crayola Crayons — the ninety-six up to the 120 — also have gel crayons. You can identify these crayons by the wrappers on them. The wrapper is black with yellow writing and reads: "Crayola Gel FX." The gel crayons are a little thicker and have wonderful bright colors. I like using them for vivid flowers and designs that I want to standout. The gel crayons can drip a little more, so try practicing with the color before you decide to use it on a project.

Glitter Crayons

There is a box of sixteen Glitter Crayons by Crayola. These make great fireworks for 4th of July-themed gourds. I also use them in flowers or to add a little sparkle to a project. Glitter crayons are just another great way to add a different look to your gourd or design.

You will find yourself using more of certain colors than others, for example, white. Lots of children do not like to use white because it does not show up on white paper. Check with your local church or schools for white crayons. You can also buy Crayola Crayons in one color. School supply stores carry individual colors or you can order them online at www.crayolastore.com. Choose from any of the Crayola colors, including the metallic crayons.

Broken crayons work well with the Wax Design. Lots of children have broken crayons they do not want, so you can use them. Another suggestion is to go to the local schools and put out a box at the end of the school year for broken crayons that are being thrown away or not wanted. People also get rid of crayons at garage sales. Crayons do not get old. They still work just fine regardless of age.

LOW TEMP MELTING POT

Low temp melting pot with well

This melting pot is UL rated. At 120°F, it is the perfect temperature for melting the crayons without getting the wax too hot. The melting pot needs to have a well in the bottom. Keeping the wax confined to this little well is what allows you to use such little crayon. The well provides an area for you to dip your wax tool into. Most melting pots are round or different shapes. You would have to use about twenty crayons to make this work in them. I have tried several other items and methods to melt my wax and have had no success.

The melting pot has a chimney on it. This is used to keep your tools warm. The melting pot is also customized so that it keeps your tool in the well.

The question that I get most often asked is, "How many melting pots do I need?" I teach you how to work with one color at a time in class so you can learn how to work with just one melting pot. The ideal number of melting pots to have is three. You are using three colors in most designs. If you are using more colors in a design, you may want more melting pots. This saves you time and money. You do not have to waste the crayon when you need a different color. If you forget a color, you do not have to refill the well to go back and apply that color. The wax can also be saved and used again later.

TEXTURE BRUSH AND INSERT

Texture Brush and Insert

The Texture Brush and Insert are designed to create textured backgrounds: trees, bushes, and grass. It also makes wonderful snow. The insert is placed on the top of the melting pot when the melting pot is empty. After the insert has warmed, melt the crayon on the insert. Use your Texture Brush to apply the crayon onto the gourd to create texture.

There is a YouTube video to help you with this process at:
http://youtu.be/qwwYk4_agoE

To clean the Texture Brush and Insert, wipe the insert while in the melting pot with a paper towel. Put the texture brush on the insert to melt the crayon. Wipe the texture brush on the paper towel. Keep repeating until the crayon is melted out. To clean the brush completely, spray with a degreaser like Awesome®. Clean again on the insert and melting pot until all of the color is gone. Rinse with warm water.

Once you have cleaned the brush, hold a paper towel folded into fours in your hand. Turn the melting pot over and put the insert onto the paper towel. Do not touch the insert. **It is very hot.** Wipe the insert with the paper towel and set the insert down to cool.

WAX DESIGN TOOLS

I have designed a line of wax tools manufactured just for this process. They each have a foam handle to keep them from getting warm while being held. The foam handle also makes them comfortable to hold. The tools are well balanced. There are three Wax Design tools. Each tool has two different size tips, so it is like getting two tools in each one.

Craft Templates MJ

The type of metal for the tools does matter. Aluminum tools will not work with this process, as aluminum does not hold the heat evenly and the wax does not stick to the tool. Wood-handled tools do not hold the heat as well either, and the wood

Wax Design Tools

handle gets very warm. A lot of thought and trial and error went into designing these tools. I have found that people who have a hard time holding other tools due to arthritis or other medical conditions find these tools easier to use. The balls on each end hold the wax on the tool.

Wax Design Tool #2 is the tool I designed first, and is still the tool I use the most. If you can only start with one tool, this is the one I recommend. It is the first tool that I start my students out with. Wax Design Tool #2 is 3/16" on one end and 1/4" on the other end. Bigger tools than this size drip a little too much.

Wax Design Tool #1 is the middle tool. It is a step down from the #2 tool. If you need a smaller stroke, this is the tool for you. Wax Design Tool #1 is 1/8" on one end and 5/32" on the other end.

Wax Design Tool #0 is the smallest of the three tools. It is used for fine detail work. It creates smaller strokes. Wax Design Tool #0 is 2/25" (2mm) on one end and 1/10" (3mm) on the other.

The size of the tool you use determines the size of the stroke or dot. If you need a bigger or longer stroke, use a bigger tool. If you need a little or short stroke or dot, use the smaller tool.

CRAFT TEMPLATES MJ®

Craft Templates MJ were invented out of, first, my frustration at not being able to create the perfect design and, second, my desire fo find a better way to create designs or trace more exact patterns. I

There is a YouTube video to show you how to use the craft templates at: *http://youtu.be/GVkHSU9VHBw*

would pull every pot, pan, bowl, and dish out of the kitchen looking for just the right size circle and then would have to get that circle onto the gourd. What if I needed that size again? Where is that circle that I used? Craft Templates MJ conform to the shape of any gourd, so you will always have the right size — any size — at your fingertips. Putting a circle onto a gourd now takes just seconds. Use them to help put the pattern on or as a guideline for cutting the top of the gourd off. Designed with gourds in mind, they are great for other crafting needs as well, such as school projects, quilting, and wood chippers. They are the first template that is flexible enough to be used on rounded or square objects, like going around a corner or on an edge of a surface. Craft Templates MJ are made of 1/16th Goodyear® rubber and come in a variety of shapes and sizes. The rubber allows them to hold in place without slipping while tracing the shape.

Circle Craft Templates MJ gives you a great variety of small to large circles. There are seven rings, all 3/8" wide, in each set. The ring sizes range from 2" to 6". These are the most common. They are also what I use the most for designs. The rings can be set inside

of one another to trace a circle within a circle, making putting on a pattern for a design very simple.

Mini Circle Craft Templates MJ are designed to give you a larger variety of smaller circles. There are eight rings in a set and the sizes range from 1" to 4". They are approximately 1/4" in width. If you do a lot of smaller work, such as Christmas ornaments, I

suggest you pick out a circle size that you want to trace and place the next size around the circle to add support to the circle. This still gives you the stable circle, but allows for a lot of smaller sizes. I use these in conjunction with the larger set if I have a circle in between a size that I want. The mini circle templates are great for putting patterns for rim designs on the gourd.

There is a YouTube video to show you how to use the templates at: http://youtu.be/T56wuHnispU

Square Craft Templates MJ and Mini Square Craft Template MJ are the same as the circles, but in the shape of squares. The square templates are not only great for making square designs, but also for making a square lid on a gourd. You can also use them for applying diamond patterns to your gourd.

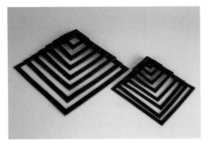

Oval Craft Templates MJ were designed because I had people telling me that they could come up with a circle and a square, but not an oval. The ovals are larger in size because most of us use them to place a pattern inside the oval. They have seven sizes, ranging from 3"

to 10". The **Mini Oval Craft Templates MJ** have eight sizes, ranging from 1.5" to 5.5". A lot of artists use them for designs on egg gourds.

There is a YouTube video to show you how to use the oval templates at: http://youtu.be/q7Zs0Rmv76w

The **Flex-e MJ®** is a flexible rubber yardstick designed to stay on the gourd without slipping. Since it is made of rubber, the ruler stays on the gourd easier than other materials. It is great for measuring gourds or mak-

ing a border. You can also use removable glue dots to help hold it in place.

There is a YouTube video to show you how to use the Flex-e at: http://youtu.be/5JZpfV-C1K8

3 POT MELTING TRAY

For safety reasons, I always work on a tray. When I was developing this method, I had six melting pots plugged in and caught the power cord as I was walking around the corner. Color went flying everywhere. It was a huge mess with all these great colors of wax in my carpet. Using a tray with a lip on it helps to keep the melting pots in place. It also keeps the wax off you and any surface you are working on. The crayon is not easy to get out of your clothes. I recommend working in an old shirt or an apron. I also designed a tray that holds the melting pots in place. This makes the melting pots more secure and less likely to move. I place the cords going away from me now, so that I am less likely to catch them.

Tray and Wax Design Tray

DRY BOARD

A dry board has little plastic spicks so that you can continue to dry your gourd after you have colored or varnished it without the gourd sticking to the board. You should not varnish on the board. This causes a build up on the dry board. Varnish the gourd first and then place it onto the board to continue drying.

Dry board with gourd on top

BASIC SUPPLIES

Removable Glue Dots are used when you need a little help holding the craft templates in place or if they are larger than what you can hold. I cut the removable glue dots in half to fit the craft template, thus making them go twice as far. Apply them to at least four places on the template, place the template on the gourd, and then trace your shape. Remove the template and pull off the glue dots. It is important to use removable glue dots — they are designed with removal in mind.

To trace the shapes for the designs, I use a **white charcoal pencil.** It leaves a bright enough line and can be removed. Unlike some of the craft pencils, you can put the charcoal pencil in the pencil sharpener to sharpen them. If the pencil is not leaving a dark enough line, simply take the pencil and use a flame from a cigarette lighter, or another type of flame, and warm the pencil tip. This makes the pencil line bright and removes any wax build-up that may have been on the pencil.

I use a **hobby knife with shovel blade** on it. Gourds are not flat. The shovel blade works better when removing wax. It also allows you to get in between strokes when removing crayon, so, if you make a mistake or have a drop of wax, you simply remove it with your hobby knife. Always use your knife at an angle. Never have the blade straight up and down. That is when scratching occurs. Start at the biggest end of the stroke or drop and work towards the small end. This allows you to get under the wax easier and you can remove more of the wax this way.

A **gum eraser** can be used to remove any wax that was left behind after you use the hobby knife. This will remove any color or stain that the crayon left in an area that you are not going over again with a stroke. I use the gum eraser more when I am working on a natural gourd that is not stained or colored. It can also be used to help clean up if you have a drop that occurred where you do not want it.

I have found that a Mr. Clean® Magic Eraser® makes removing the charcoal pencil lines easy — these can be found in the bathroom cleaning supplies of most stores. I cut my sponge into three sections; it is a little easier to use this way and last a little longer. Wet it slightly and wring out the water. Wipe the area that has the charcoal pencil. This will leave a chalky white film behind. Lightly dampen a paper towel and remove this film.

There is a YouTube video to help you with this process at: **http://youtu.be/voGnUzpENYI**

I keep a container of water on my tray so that I do not have to get up and get water. Use a small plastic container instead of glass so that it does not break. The water is used to wet your Magic Eraser, sea sponge, or cotton swab. Water is needed for painting cleanup too.

Of course, the most important items are the cleanup items. They make cleaning up a breeze. **Cotton Balls** are used to absorb the crayon and clean the melting pot. **Q-Tips®**, or cotton swabs, are used to clean the chimney if the crayon gets into it. Damped Q-Tips can also be used to remove charcoal pencil lines in hard to get to areas. **Paper towels** are used to wipe and clean your Wax Design Tools, as well as help clean the texture brush and insert. **Cotton Rounds** are used to apply dye to the gourd.

STAINS, DYES, PAINTS, AND VARNISHES

All kinds of dyes, stains, and paints can be used on gourds. I have tried to test as many as possible to make sure they work well with this process. The only method of coloring that I would not use with Wax Design is shoe polish or anything with wax in it, as wax does not like to go over other wax.

One of my favorite dyes are **alcohol inks.** They are easy to apply. No matter what you do, they seem to come out great. With a large variety of colors, you have lots of choices and can create great color combinations.

Leather dyes come in a variety of colors as well, but they have a tendency to fade. I will use leather dye as a base to get a rich base and then apply ink dye or alcohol dye over it to keep it from fading as much.

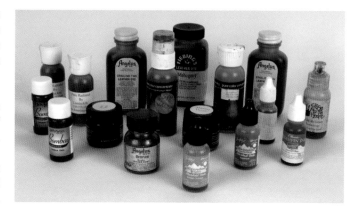

When doing a black gourd, I will only use acrylic paint. The other dyes will spot over time. I do a lot of sponging on the gourd for texture and background with the acrylic paint. Metallic acrylic paint is a great background for Christmas ornament gourds.

Applying a basecoat of acrylic paint and then using a dye on top of that really brings out the color of the dye and makes a nice contrast. Remember when applying colors, such as blue and green, that the gourd has a yellow base, which will affect these colors. If you want true blues or greens, you may want to apply a white base first. This can be done with white acrylic, gesso, or a white dye. Apply your color over that. This method also makes colors brighter and more vibrant.

VARNISH, GLAZE, AND LACQUER

For the wax design process, I prefer Krylon® gloss spray, which is a non-yellowing varnish. The price is right and you can find it at

most stores. I like using the Krylon® Triple Thick glaze for a better protective coat when I know that a gourd is going to be handled more. However, if you already have a favorite, I am sure it will work just fine.

You can also use a brush-on varnish or polyurethane. When using a brush-on, you need to make sure that your color is set and will not run when it is applied. For Christmas ornaments, to give it more protection, I use Deco Art® Triple Thick brush-on. Remember to always test your products on a small area of the surface you plan to use the finish on. I test mine on the bottom of my gourd that will not show. The manufacturers are always changing formulas, so testing a small area assures that you are happy with the finish on your surface.

CLEANING YOUR WAX DESIGN TOOLS

To clean the color off your wax tools, simply wipe your tool with a paper towel when it is warm. It is much harder to do if the wax has cooled. Place it back into the well and warm it up again. I keep my paper towel folded in fours and in the right front corner of my tray.

CLEANING YOUR MELTING POT

To change colors or clean your melting pot, simply take a cotton ball and pull it in half. Keep it in balls. Take the first half and place it in the well. I like to use the smallest Wax Design Tool #0 because it can get into the tight corners. Do not touch the metal with your fingers. The metal is hot! Using the tool, slowly push it into the

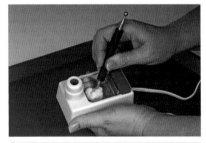

There is a YouTube video to help you with this process at: http://youtu.be/FKQKi-Y9lhs

well. If you push the cotton ball in too fast, the color comes out the sides, making a bigger mess. Going slower allows the wax to absorb as it goes. Lift it out with your wax tool. Start at the front of the well,

get under the cotton ball, and pull it out. Take the second piece of the cotton ball and start by cleaning the top of the well with your wax tool. Finish by cleaning inside the well. You will be amazed how easy it is to clean. The cleaning is done while the melting pot is plugged in. Once you have cleaned the well, put your new color in to melt.

The crayon can be left in the well and used again later. Just plug the melting pot back in when you are ready to use it again and wait for it to melt before you start. If you were done with the color, unplug the melting pot and let the color cool. When the wax

is hard, plug the melting pot back in. It will start to melt on the sides. Take you hobby knife and pop the color out. You will get a small block of wax that you can use for next time. Just drop it into the well when you are ready to use. If needed, add more crayon to fill the well.

If you happen to put your Wax Design Tool back in the chimney without cleaning the wax first or if you noticed that your tool is picking up wax while in the chimney, then take a Q-Tip and clean out the chimney. Try to remember to wipe your tools off before putting them into the chimney.

A copper wire scouring pad is used to clean the outside of the gourd.

CLEANING AND CUTTING THE GOURD

Gourds grow with a waxy "skin" that must be removed. The skin is often moldy and dirty. If the skin is not removed, your wax will not "stick" nor will a finish coat sealer. It will look good now, but in six months or so it will start peeling and chipping. If you have a gourd that has not been cleaned, you will need to soak it in warm water and clean it with a copper wire scourer. Once you've cleaned them, allow them to dry. You can also buy gourds that are already cleaned, as well as cut, from some gourd farmers. This is nice if you want to buy them ready-to-go. **Please use mold precautions, such as wearing a mask, and make sure there is adequate ventilation in the area when cleaning and handling unclean gourds.** Some people have mold allergies.

There is a YouTube video to help you with this process at:
http://youtu.be/EqOIZs_45Rs

SAND OR NOT TO SAND

For the Wax Design process, I feel it is **not** better to sand the gourd unless there are scratches or blemishes on it. If there are some, then sand using fine-grade sandpaper on those areas to remove the flaws. However, the less you sand the gourd, the more the wax has to adhere to.

CUTTING THE GOURD

One way to cut a gourd is to use a jigsaw. First, you need to make the line where you are going to cut the gourd. You can use the craft templates to help assist you in this. Trace the line on with the white charcoal pencil. To start the cut, drill a hole into the gourd or make a hole with your hobby knife. Once you have made the hole, insert the blade of your jigsaw. To keep the jigsaw from kicking back, keep pressure against the gourd. Saw the line that you placed on the gourd. Continue until you reach the place where you started. If you like, you can sand the cut rim to make it smooth. You can also use a Dremel® tool or a hobby knife to cut the gourd.

There is a YouTube video to help you with this process at:
http://youtu.be/MOtPvlMsWhE

CLEANING AND SPRAY-PAINTING THE INSIDE OF THE GOURD

Remove any large parts that are loose. Use the scraper to clean the inside of the gourd. Start at the bottom of the gourd and pull up to the top with the scraper. Continue around until you have cleaned the whole gourd.

There is a YouTube video to help you with this process at:
http://youtu.be/S5Z5-gtB_qY

Color the inside of the gourd with black spray-paint. I use the least inexpensive can of black spray-paint that I can find. I use gloss, but flat is fine as well. Shake the spray-paint to mix it. Use latex gloves when spraying to keep the paint off your hands. Hold the can inside the gourd. Do not pull it pass the rim. This is the one time that you can spray closer. The inside of the gourd is very absorbent and it goes on well. Spray the bottom and the sides. Do not try to spray the rim. This is when over-spray gets on the gourd. If you do get over-spray on your rim, dampen your Magic Eraser and rub until the paint is removed.

If the gourd is too tall and you cannot reach the bottom of the gourd with the paint, take black acrylic paint and water it down. Pour it into the gourd and swish it around. Make sure that you do not use too much paint because you do not want to have to pour the paint out. It makes a mess and will get on the outside of the gourd. Use only enough to cover and absorb into the gourd. Paint the rim with black acrylic paint.

I do not like to use spray-paint on the outside of my gourd. The paint can sometimes bubble and it is a different texture to work on.

There is a YouTube video to help you with this process at:
http://youtu.be/1luE0u08eoc

COLORING AND VARNISHING THE GOURD

Apply dye to the gourd using a cotton round. I have tried to test as many colors, paints, and dyes as I can get my hands onto. Refer back to the section on stains, dyes, paints, and varnishes on page 12. If you are applying acrylic paint, you need to basecoat the gourd with at least two coats of paint. If it is a thin color, which requires several layers, you may want to start with a basecoat of gesso.

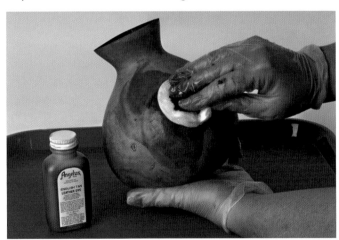

There is a YouTube video to help you with this process at:
http://youtu.be/FU98nGAUi_8

When applying leather dye, to keep areas from getting lighter or darker due to absorption of the gourd, take a damp paper towel and rub the gourd. This will make the dye apply more evenly. Otherwise, the gourd may have areas that are more absorbent and less absorbent — this equals it out. It also helps to make it less streaky. Shake the leather dye well. I always use latex gloves when I am dyeing a gourd. Using a cotton round, I put the color in the middle of it and start from the bottom of my gourd, going in circles. When I reach the sides, I go back and forth. Apply more dye if the dye starts to lighten up. You can apply more than one coat if you like.

When using ink or alcohol dyes, there is no need to dampen the gourd. These dyes do not streak. I apply them using the same method.

I work on a tray when I am dyeing or staining gourds. I have spilled the dye too many times. By working on a tray, it keeps a spill from becoming a disaster.

SPRAY-VARNISHING THE GOURD

If you have used leather dye or if you are working on a gourd stained or painted black, you can spray a light coat of Krylon on now, before you start to decorate it. This is done for several reasons: If you are using leather dye, it will help keep the paint from getting all over you. If you're working on a black-colored gourd, it helps keep the black clean and from picking up wax pieces. It also makes it easier to remove the charcoal pencil lines, and will seal the base color to prevent bleeding through to future color layers.

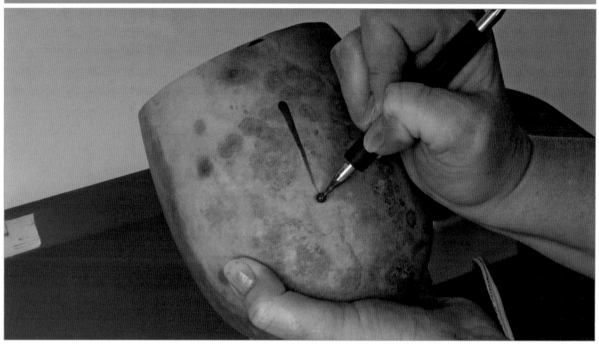

SETTING UP YOUR TRAY

Set your low temp melting pot in the right-hand corner of your tray if you are right-handed and on the left if you are left-handed. If you drip, chances are the drip will land on the tray. Place the well so that the chimney is in the back. The cord will be in the front. Place the cords away from you to keep from getting tangled in them. I use a power strip to keep the melting pots plugged in so that I do not have to unplug all of the melting pots individually — I can just flip the switch to turn them off. I place my paper towel folded into fours on the right lower side. I keep my water container in the left top corner, where I am less likely to hit and spill it. Tools and crayons are kept close to the front for easy reach.

Tray set up with a Wax Design tray.

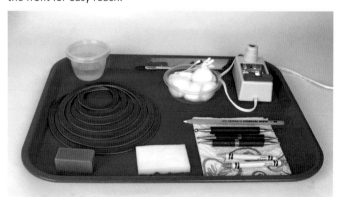

Tray set up with a regular tray.

ADDING YOUR CRAYON

The first thing you need to do is plug in your low temp melting pot and get it warmed up. This only takes a few minutes, and you can load your crayon while it's warming. Remember to use only Crayola crayons. (See "Using and Melting Crayola Crayons" on page 8). I also refer to Crayola crayon as wax, which is what it is. Holding the crayon with the tip pointed towards the top, cut the crayon just above the word "Crayola."

With your hobby knife, cut the paper down the side of the crayon to where you first cut the paper. Do not try to peel the paper back with the knife. It is much harder that way and you are more likely to cut yourself.

Peel the paper off the crayon to where you cut it with the hobby knife. I leave the rest of the paper on my crayon. This keeps it clean and from getting other colors on the crayon. I also leave the name as the last part of the crayon to use so if I need to know what color I need, I have that information.

With your hands, break the crayon down to the paper. Break that piece again and add both pieces into the well part of your melting pot. By breaking the crayon into two pieces, this keeps it from melting on the top layer of the well and wasting your crayon.

It is okay to get some of the crayon on the next level of the well — it just helps to keep it cleaner and avoids waste to keep the crayon in the well. Allow your crayon to melt all the way. When it has melted, you will know that it's ready to use.

*There is a YouTube video you can watch that shows you how to cut and add the crayon at: **http://youtu.be/64wt_GAWB3s***

Your melted crayon should not overflow into the second level. You want to make sure that you do not fill the well too full. If the well is so full that you cannot see the rectangle of the well, you will start to drip more. If you filled the well too full, simply take a cotton ball and absorb a little of the crayon.

*There is a YouTube video to help you know if you have too much crayon in the well at: **http://youtu.be/S6bcOZJ0IZg***

Keep the well full by adding more crayon as needed. Using your hobby knife, cut the crayon with the paper still on it. It is important to keep your well full. Do not let your well get less than three-quarters full. This keeps your strokes the same size

because you are picking up the same amount of wax. To add crayon to your well, take your hobby knife and cut the size of crayon piece you may need. Lay the crayon on your tray and cut down onto the tray. Do not cut it in your hand — that does not end well. I leave the paper on when I am doing this. A lot of times once it is cut it comes out of the paper all by itself; if not, then cut the paper with your hobby knife and remove.

*There is a YouTube video to help you know when to add more crayon to your well at: **http://youtu.be/LBQatFU1dnY***

LOADING YOUR TOOL

Warm your tools by placing them in the wax or keeping them warm in the chimney of the melting pot. **This is the most important information to make this process work.** If you do not warm your tools and try to apply warm wax with a cold tool, you will get

a glob of wax. The wax will stick to the tool and not want to come off. It only takes about fifteen seconds or more to warm the tool. If the area you are working in is cooler, the tool may take a few seconds longer to warm.

Make sure that the gourd you are working on is not cold. Do not run out to the shed in the winter time and grab a gourd and start applying wax. The gourd needs to warm to room temperature.

Place your tool in the deepest part of the well and pull straight up. Start with the Wax Design Tool #2 small end. This is the easier of the tools to begin with. Place it into your wax and warm the end of your tool. Once your Wax Design Tool is warm, place it in

the deepest part of the well. Go all the way to the bottom. Touch the bottom and pull your tool straight out. By pulling it straight up, you get the maximum amount of wax. Do not pull the tool out slowly or come up along the sides of the well. This removes some of the wax.

There is a YouTube video to help you with this process at:
http://youtu.be/7TWjiINf3kQ

Watch yourself the first few times you load your strokes, as it is instinct to want to knock off the drip of wax. **You want the drip. The drip is what adds texture to your stroke.** You will not even know that you are doing this. Be careful not to form bad habits of stirring it, clicking the sides, or hitting it. The crayon should only be stirred if it has been sitting awhile and the color has separated in the wax. White crayons need stirring a little more, as do metallic and glitter crayons. The easiest way to do this process is not to over think it. Just go to the deepest part of the well, touch the bottom, and pull straight out for your stroke. Make sure you load in the same spot each time, as this will keep your strokes consistent. Know where you are going with your stroke before you pick it up. Do not load the wax and sit there and hold it while you are looking where to go. This cools your wax and your strokes do not go on smooth. Also, it is natural to get excited after putting on a stroke — while still holding the tool in your hand. Watch out for this. I am the worst offender of holding the tool in my hand while talking to someone.

To keep it warm, your tool can be kept in the chimney when you are not using it. Your Wax Design Tool should not need to be warmed as long as you are going from the wax to making a stroke and back to the wax. Keep the gourd no

further than 12" from the melting pot. Any further and your tool starts to cool off. Keep different size tools in the chimney of the melting pot, so that they are ready to be used. You can also keep the tool in the wax of another melting pot. You can use these tools when you need them without waiting for them to warm up.

PRACTICING YOUR STROKES

Hold your tool like you would a pencil — to the side with your hand resting on the gourd. Pick up a pencil and hold it in your hand as if you were going to write something. Notice how you hold your pencil sideways while resting the side of your

hand on the paper. This is how you should hold your tool. By resting it on the side of your hand, this gives you control of your stoke. Do not try to hold your tool straight up and down or try to balance it with your little finger. You will have no control over your stroke and will not get straight lines if you hold your tool up-straight without resting you hand on the gourd for control.

Pull your stroke straight down towards you. Pull it until your wax tool runs out of wax. Practice your strokes on gourd shards (pieces of gourds) or a piece of paper. Load your tool with wax and bring it to the gourd and set it down. With your hand sideways — like you would hold a pencil — and your hand resting on the gourd, pull the stroke toward

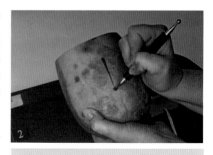

There is a YouTube video to help you with this process at: **http://youtu.be/ imRRnLwBdkw**

you. Like brush work, you should pull your strokes directly toward you. Load and set the tool on the gourd, pulling it until it runs out of wax. Most people lift the tool too early. Pull, pull, pull that stroke. You are starting with a bunch of wax and going until there is no wax left on the tool. Allowing it to pull until it runs out will result in a great tail on the stroke.

Make sure that you are pulling your stroke nice and easy. Do not skim the top of the gourd with the tool. Set it on the gourd and pull your stroke nice and slow. Pulling it too fast makes the wax skip. The slower you pull the stroke, the longer the stroke becomes. Remember that the length and width of the stroke is controlled by the size of the tools you use: the bigger the tool, the bigger the stroke; the smaller the tool, the smaller the stroke. **You must reload for each stroke.** You want to run

out of wax with your tool. As soon as the wax turns from shining to dull, it is dry. It dries within seconds. This is great because you do not get your hands in wet wax. Since the wax dries so fast, you cannot go over a stroke if you do not like it. The wax is already cold and it will just make a mess.

There is a YouTube video to help you with this process at:
http://youtu.be/PH8tSEQYBJ0

If you notice that the edges of your stroke are uneven or are not smooth, you need to warm your tool a little more. When you are working with wax, a breeze or air circulation can affect it. If you are working in front of a fan, an open window, or the furnace in

the winter, this can make the wax drip more. Make sure that the gourd you are working on is at room temperature and not damp. This will also affect the wax.

Dots and descending dots. Dots are loaded the same as a stroke. Do not think that because it is a dot you can dip it anywhere. The size of the tools determines the size of the dots. Load the tool each time and make a dot. Make sure you go to the bottom of the well when loading the wax. If you don't, your dots will not

There is a YouTube video to help you with this process at:
http://youtu.be/7fGqF5YDpMI

end up the same size. You can also do a descending dot, which is a lot of fun. Load your tool and dot, dot, dot. Each dot will be smaller because you are running out of wax. I use this method a lot in my designs. You can do a design with just dots. There are a lot of paisley designs that use only dots. You will also notice little tiny flecks of wax when you add the dots. More flecks for larger dots. This is just part of it. If you are getting more than two flecks per dot, then slow

down. You can remove them with your hobby knife. I leave them in depending on if I want more texture to my design.

REMOVING A STROKE OR DROP

With your hobby knife, remove a stroke, dot, or drop you do not want. Always start at the fat end of the stroke. I am working with the shovel tip on the hobby knife. Gourds are not flat. The shovel nose lets you get in between your strokes and only remove

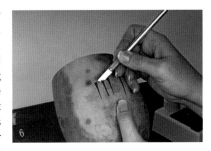

the stroke you want. Allow the wax to dry. Trying to remove it while it is wet is harder and can smear the color of the crayon, making a bigger mess to clean up and staining the gourd.

Put the hobby knife under the largest part of the stroke or drop. Starting with the largest part of the stroke will get a bigger piece of the wax off. Hold the hobby knife at an angle. Do not hold the knife up and down or scratches will occur. Turn the knife to the other angle to remove the tail part of the stroke. If you need to remove any stain left behind from the wax, especially if you are working on a natural gourd, then use your gum eraser and it will clean right up.

There is a YouTube video to help you with this process at:
http://youtu.be/fGNg21bfb2A

PRACTICE MAKES PERFECT

You should practice until you are comfortable with your strokes, dots, and removing a mistake. Try different tools to make different size strokes and dots. Some people find that a certain size Wax Design Tool works better or is easier for them to use. Make sure you try both ends of each Wax Design Tool. Know that each Crayola crayon will work differently. The darker colors, or colors with more pigment, will make bigger strokes because they are thicker. The thinner colors, such as green-yellow, will be thin, but will pull further. Know how the color that you want to use works. Thinner colors will drip a little more. I take the colors that I will be using and pull them with each tool so that I know how long that color will pull or what size the stroke will be.

Practice in each of the colors you want to use so that you are familiar with how that color works. Practice until your strokes become consistent in size. The more you practice, the better your strokes will become. Remember that you are your own worst critic. If you do not like a stroke, then remove it. If it bugs you, then take it off.

There is a YouTube video to help you with this process at:
http://youtu.be/cR5Tmi-kJ5E

4

The designs mentioned in this chapter are just my designs that I offer you as a guide, a springboard for creating your own designs. Please remember to not get stuck in my designs. Think about what you can create on your own. What shapes can you mix and match to make a great design? How can you add pulled out strokes and dots to complete that design? What rim decoration would complement that gourd? Use the information that I give you to start your own wonderful adventure.

CIRCLE

Using the circle craft templates, trace the inside of the smallest circle onto your practice gourd or shard with a white charcoal pencil. Place a dot in the center of the circle. This gives you a reference point.

You will be pulling your strokes from the outside of the circle to the center dot. Use the small end of Wax Design Tool #1 for this size circle. Start at the top of the circle and pull the first stroke towards the middle. The stroke should be at the 12 o'clock position. Pretend you are looking at the face of a clock. Make sure that you are pulling the stroke towards you. Turn the gourd upside-down so that the bottom is now the top. Pull your stroke again from the top to the center. Do not worry if the strokes do not make it all the way

to the center; what matters is whether you have run out of wax and it is consistent in size with the other strokes. You will be adding embellishments to the center of the circles after you have created a design. This really cleans up the tails and fills in the empty areas. Turn the gourd half way to the side so that the stroke will be at the top. This stroke would be at the 3 o'clock position on your circle. Pull the stroke to the middle. Now, turn the gourd so that the 9 o'clock position is on top. Pull the stroke to the middle. This will give you the four points of your circle. I always quarter off my designs. This helps the patterns so they are more even.

Now, come back in between each of the strokes and add another set of strokes, making a total of eight strokes. Start at your right and work clockwise so you do not lose your place. Add another set of strokes in between each stroke, leaving you with a total of sixteen strokes. Do not look at the design — break it down into sections or quarters — and do not get overwhelmed. If you can cut pie, you can do this! It is as easy as cutting pie!

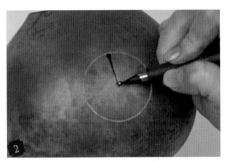

Start at the 12:00 position and pull to the center dot or until your wax tool runs out of wax.

Turn the gourd so the 3:00 position is straight up and pull the stroke to the center dot.

Now that you have quartered your design, go back and pull a stroke in between each of the four strokes for a total of eight strokes.

Flip the gourd over and repeat the previous step.

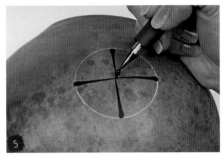

Turn the gourd again, so the 9:00 position is on top. Pull the stroke to the center dot.

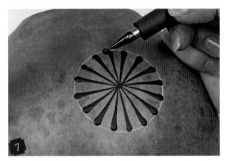

Go back in between the strokes one more time for a total of sixteen strokes.

There is a YouTube video to help you with this process at:
http://youtu.be/wNQvvIkTOQ8

DOUBLE CIRCLE

To create a double circle, take the smallest and the second smallest sizes of the circle craft templates and lay them one inside of the other and then trace the inside circle with your charcoal pencil. Remove that circle. Trace the inside of the bigger circle. By setting the circles inside of each other, the circles are already lined up.

Pull your strokes from the outside circle in between the inside circle until you reach the center or run out of wax on your tool. Starting with the smaller circle and using the small end of Wax Design Tool #1, add your strokes until you have sixteen strokes, creating the smaller circle. Change to the small end of Wax Design Tool #2. Start on the outside circle and pull strokes in between each of the smaller strokes. Yes, the strokes will fit. More of the wax will come off before you get to the smaller size strokes, allowing you room to pull in between the other strokes. Pull them to the center of the circle or until you run out of wax. It is okay to run out of wax. Follow your circle around in a clockwise direction until you have completed the circle.

SQUARE

Counting out from the middle of the square craft templates, trace the inside of the third square onto the gourd with your charcoal pencil. Place a dot with your charcoal pencil in the middle of your square. Starting with the square corners and using the small end of Wax Design Tool #2, pull your stroke to the center dot or until you run out of wax. Do all four corners. Come back and do a stroke in the middle of the four strokes that you just completed, making a total of eight strokes. Divide the square just like you did the circle. Think of it as a square pie.

Pull a stroke from all four corners until you reach the center or run out of wax.

Working clockwise, add a stroke in between each of the eight strokes. This will make a total of sixteen strokes. You should have room to add one more set of strokes to the square, making a total of thirty-two strokes. At first you will not think that you have room to add the strokes, but by adding more strokes it makes the texture that much better and fills in the color. Do not be afraid to get the strokes in. If you get to the first eight strokes on and know there is no room for three more strokes in between each set of strokes, then you can do two strokes in between each stroke.

Pull a stroke in the middle of the four strokes that you just completed.

Work clockwise so you do not lose your place. Put another set of strokes in between the eight strokes for a total of sixteen strokes.

There is a YouTube video to help you with this process at: **http://youtu.be/ z9XtpbvpBME**

You will have room for one more set of strokes. It will be tight, but this is what gives it such great texture.

PUTTING TWO SQUARES TOGETHER

Two squares together form a small square where they meet. Create a new design by putting two squares together. Have the squares meet at the middle to form a smaller square. Counting out from the middle

of the square craft templates, trace the inside of the fourth square. Lay the template on the right corner of the first square until you line up a small square — this would be where the two squares meet and should be in the center of the first square. Trace on the inside of the square.

Starting with the square on the left, pull strokes from the three corners to the middle. Repeat this on the square on the right.

On the left side, come back in and add strokes in between these strokes. Repeat on the right square.

On the left side, outside of the little square, pull a stroke on each side to the middle of the big square. Repeat on the right square.

On the left side, add a stroke in between each of the strokes on the square for a total of thirteen strokes. Repeat on the right square. Remember that if three strokes will not fit into this area you can do a total of two strokes and be done with the square.

On the left side, go back and add one more set of strokes in between each of the strokes in the square. Repeat on the right square. You should have a total of twenty-five strokes.

With black crayon, create a small square in the middle of the design. Switch to the large end of Wax Design Tool #0. Working on the little square, start at the four corners and pull to the middle. Put strokes in between the four strokes for a total of eight strokes. If you have room, you can divide and add one more set of strokes for a total of sixteen.

PUTTING SHAPES TOGETHER

Apply pattern using the circle and square templates. Create new designs by putting different shapes together. Take the smallest of the circle templates and, using a charcoal pencil, trace on the inside of the circle. Counting from the middle of the square templates, find the fifth ring. Place this so that the circle is in the middle of the square and trace the square on the inside of the template.

Apply pattern using the square and oval templates. Let's start with the square this time. Counting from the middle of the square templates, select the third square and trace it in the middle with your charcoal pencil. Now grab your oval craft templates and count from the middle to find the second oval. Trace half the oval on each of the four sides of the square.

Design completed, using a circle and a square together. Using the steps that we have already gone over, create your circle with sixteen strokes. On your square, start at the outside corners and pull the strokes until you get to the circle or you run out of wax. Start dividing the square off and adding more strokes — add as many strokes as you think the square needs. Start to understand how you can mix and match your shapes. You may need more or less strokes to complete the design.

Design completed, using a square and an oval together. Start adding strokes to your square by dividing it off. Fill up the square with strokes until you feel your design is complete. Now, start at the center of the oval, pulling the stroke until you meet the square or run out of wax. Start the second stroke above the square and pull the stroke until you get to the middle of the oval. Repeat on the other side. Start to divide the oval off. Keep adding strokes until you feel that you have completed the design.

PULLING STROKES OUT

Pull strokes out of the square designs where the square dips or on the corners. Again, this adds so much more to the design. It opens it up and completes the design. You can do a couple of these or add as many as you feel the design needs.

You can add to your designs by pulling strokes out from the shape. Take the double circles and, just above the smaller strokes, start your new strokes and pull them out. Make sure to turn the gourd so that you are pulling the stroke towards you. Let the wax run out on its own. Do not lift the tool up until the wax has run out. This keeps the strokes close to the same size. Pulling the strokes out really opens up the design.

Pulling strokes out where the ovals dip. Pull the strokes out of the oval design in the same way as you did the square design. Pull it from the dips in the design. This also helps to fill out the design.

DOTS

At my house, I call these **"happy dots."** Dots make me happy. I think that dots add so much visual pleasure to a design. It seems to just really pull a design together and complete it. Dots can be used on top of a stroke to make a point or clean up stroke ends. Do not put a dot in the middle of a design if you plan to glue an embellishment there. If you are not planning on using embellishments, then you can use a dot in the center of your design.

Dots added to every other stroke on square.

Dots added to end of pulled strokes to clean up ends.

Descending dots are fun and help to fill in the areas between the strokes. Depending on the tool that you are using and the wax, you can do three or more dots without reloading. Keep the dots the same in number.

Dots added to the points of squares.

Descending dots added above the turquoise strokes completes the design and makes it stand out.

There is a YouTube video to help you with this process at: **http://youtu.be/7fGqF5YDpMI**

24

RIM DESIGNS

You can make great rim designs using the wax technique. One of my favorite designs on the rim is half circles. Divide the gourd into four sections so you can figure out what size of circles you need for that area. You can also mark on your circle templates with a charcoal pencil so you can remove the line later. Mark

Using a charcoal pencil, trace half of the mini circle craft template to create a pattern for the rim. Mark a small dot in the center of the half circle next to the rim.

the circle in half, and place the circle onto the rim of the gourd. Line the rim up with the lines on the circle. Trace the inside of the circle. Do this again until you have the half circles traced on the rim of the gourd. Add a dot to the center of the half circles right next to the rim.

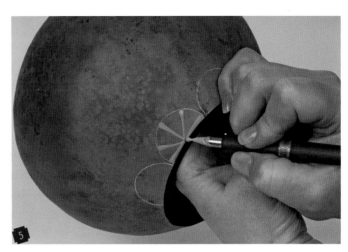

Turn the gourd upside-down so that the half circle is on top. Pull the stroke from the center of the half circle to the dot.

Pull the next stroke from the left side of the circle to the dot. This is just above the rim.

Pull the stroke from the right side, again just above the rim, to the dot.

Divide the area between the strokes with another stroke. Add another stroke if you have room. You can leave the rim like this or you can add a dot above each stroke.

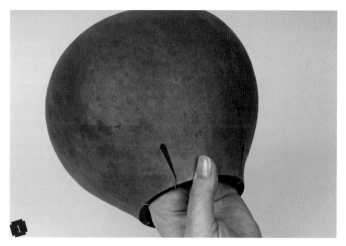

To create a descending rim, divide the gourd into eight sections, or more if you have a larger rim. Do a long stroke every other section.

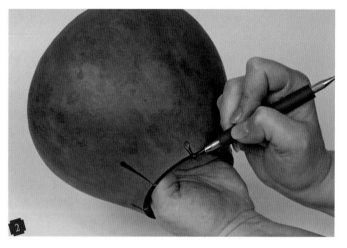

Do a short stroke on the sections that are left.

Come back in the middle of the two stokes and do a stroke half the length.

Divide it two more times if you have room. If you can only get two strokes in between each of the strokes, then do that.

You can add dots anywhere you think they are needed to add to the rim design.

You can even pull some strokes down from the top to add more to the design.

You can create a rim by using random size strokes and dots. Start with your first color, leaving room for two more colors. Place random size strokes on the gourd, pulling towards the rim. Switch to your second color. Remember to allow for one more color. Pull towards the rim. It is okay to fall off the rim. Once you have gone around the rim, switch to your third color. Fill in the remaining strokes. Once you've completed this, come back and add dots or descending dots to one or more of the colors.

Change colors by dyeing and add fun fur to create a new look. This method is covered in the Projects chapter under "Peacock in Moonlight," starting on page 32.

Embellishments add so much to a design. They help to clean-up the tails, can make the design complete, or fill in open areas. There are so many wonderful things that you can use for embellishments. When selecting my embellishments, I am looking for color, size, and a flat side. The embellishments are easier to glue on if they have a flat side. You want a color that sets off your design.

BEADS

Beads are the most common embellishment. There are lots of beads. Silver beads make a nice center when working with a smaller design. I use a lot of turquoise stones because of my style and Southwest influence. Flat coral stones are wonderful as well. Shell beads are often flat and come in lots of colors that are affordable. Black-cut shiny beads are a must for your embellishment collection. I look for beads when I am at a yard sale or thrift store. This is a great way to find wonderful beads for less money. Don't forget you can use beads that are already in a necklace — a simple snip with the scissors provides tons of embellishments from a single purchase.

STONES

Stones make great decorations for wax design. The great thing about stones is that you can get them in all kinds of shapes and colors. This gives you a bigger variety of embellishments. You can also get fancier stones like cabochons, which are flat on the back. There are also cabochons with feathers around them.

RHINESTONES AND GEMS

Rhinestones are great to use to add that extra sparkle to your design. They are great because they are light and flat, making them easy to glue on. Rhinestones are really big right now and you can find them in all types of designs and shapes. Add them to Christmas ornaments you have created using the Wax Design to give it that Christmas spirit or if you just have someone who likes "bling."

There are all kinds of things out there that would look great in the center of your design. It could be something from nature, a memento that was something special to a loved one, an old piece of jewelry, or one earring without a partner. Add a sinker or fish lure to make the design more masculine. Think outside the box and make this gourd special.

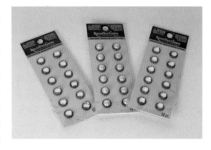

GLUING ON EMBELLISHMENTS

When gluing on embellishments, I only use E6000®. You can find it in most stores in the craft section or in the glue section. It is epoxy glue, which means you can glue tough items like rocks, stones, or glass. The texture is not as runny as I would like

it. You also have to put a toothpick down the opening to get it flowing when using it again, but once you glue that embellishment on, it is going to stay on. When applying the glue, less is better. I use a toothpick to apply the glue. Put the glue onto the embellishment — not the gourd. The glue will leave a tail, much like glue from a hot glue gun, and you do not want that on the gourd. Make sure that you did not apply so much glue that it comes out from under the embellishment.

I take wax paper and wipe the top of the glue before putting the cap back on. This helps to keep it clean and makes it easier to get the lid off the next time you use it. Once you have applied the embellishment onto your gourd, watch that it does not slide. Watch the embellishment for at least thirty minutes. So many people will watch it for awhile, walk away, and then the embellishment slides. The heavier the embellishment, the more likely the embellishment will slide. Holding the embellishment in place for a few minutes helps. Laying the gourd so that the embellishment is straight up will also help.

There is a YouTube video to help you with this process at:
http://youtu.be/ykBCyMRzBEI

SCRAPBOOK EMBELLISHMENTS

I love getting embellishments from the scrapbook section. You have a wide selection and all kinds of colors and designs. They are lightweight and have flat backs. Most of them have a sticky back, but you can still add your glue to them. I really like the pearls. You can also find flat silver, copper, and gold dots. During the holidays, use holiday-themed embellishments to make your designs more special.

BRADS

Brads are not the plain old brads that we used in school to bring our paper artwork to life. I found that they come in large selections and are bigger than the scrapbook embellishments. This makes them perfect for the center of your design. Take your wire cutters and cut off your brads before gluing them onto your gourd. With these beautiful designs, no one would ever imagine that these embellishments were ever a brad.

Varnish, spray varnish, glaze, lacquer

SPRAY-ON VARNISH

A lot of people are intimidated by spray varnishes. Do not let varnishes worry you — just try it. Practice on gourd shards to get comfortable. Runs are caused by being too close or going too slow when varnishing. Varnish in a ventilated area. If you are working outside in the sun, remember that you are working with wax and *you cannot leave it in the sun to dry.*

Start by shaking your can to mix the varnish. Spray about 12" away from the gourd. Start at the bottom of the gourd and spray in a circular motion. Do the sides of the gourd, starting at the top and going to the bottom in a back and forth motion at a medium speed. Do not use a circular motion when doing the sides. It does not cover evenly. Go back and forth until you have sprayed the entire gourd. Place the gourd on a dry board so that it can continue drying without sticking to the bottom of the board. If you are doing a bowl, you might want to turn it upside down to dry. Once the varnish is dry to touch, apply another coat. Applying varnish not only protects the wax, but also brings out the color. Apply at least two to three coats.

The humidity can cause your varnish to turn white. This can also happen at night because, again, it is more humid. This is why I like to use Krylon Gloss. It is less likely to turn white. If your varnish should turn white, let it dry and varnish it again on a drier day to turn it back. *Remember that this is wax so do not apply heat of any type.*

There is a YouTube video to help you with this process at:
http://youtu.be/vfS2XTm2mzY

BRUSH-ON VARNISH

You can use Brush-on varnish if you have used acrylic paint or have heat set your dyes. Brush-on varnish can pick the dye or color up and bring it over your wax, so make sure that, when using it, your color is heat set. I will use a brush-on varnish over a spray varnish to create more protection for the wax. Make sure that you have spray-varnished well, so that the color does not come up when the brush-on varnish is applied. Since the products are always changing, when mixing products, always do a test section on the bottom of the gourd to make sure that you have no problems with them.

GLAZES

I like to work with a glaze to add a thicker layer to help the wax be more durable. When working with Christmas ornaments that are going to be handled, I use Triple Thick brush-on by DecoArt. I basecoat the ornaments in acrylic paint or metallic acrylics so they will not bleed when the glaze is applied. Apply at least three coats of glaze to the ornament. The more coats you apply, the more durable the wax becomes. I also apply this over a design after it has been varnished, for more protection. This is a water-based product so you can add water to it if it becomes too thick. Stir it very well.

LACQUER

Lacquer can also be used to seal your gourd. When working with jewelry that is going to be worn out in the sun and would otherwise melt, I use 3D Crystal Lacquer® Thick. Straight out of the bottle, start at the center of your piece and work your way to the outside. Use this in small areas where you can keep the gourd piece flat. This will go on very thick and will cover all of the wax and will be white in color until the lacquer dries. This product takes awhile to dry. Make sure that you do not move it during this time. Lacquer can also be applied by brushing it on. Allow to dry and apply more layers until you get the desired coverage. I would do at least three or more coats. It is also water-based so you can clean your brush with warm water and soap.

There are always new products coming out. I am always testing and experimenting with products. Find a product that works well for you and will protect the wax. Do not be afraid to try new items.

I do new videos with the new items that I may be working with on my You-Tube site at: *http://www.youtube.com/user/Miriamjoy123?feature=mhee*

PEACOCK IN THE MOONLIGHT

SUPPLY LIST

Gourd • turquoise leather dye • purple leather dye • black acrylic paint • black spray paint • paintbrushes • low temp melting pot • Wax Design Tools #2 and #1 • charcoal pencil • circle craft templates • blue-green and white Crayola crayons, • spray varnish • turquoise embellishment • feathers • E6000 • toothpicks • tray • hobby knife • paper towels • cotton balls and cotton rounds • latex gloves • water container • Mr. Clean Magic Eraser • hot glue gun • turquoise leather or suede lacing • dry board

Once you have mastered the basic strokes, you can start to have some fun and make wonderful projects. Let's begin with a simple design and add some great embellishments. This project is intended to show you how wonderful "simple" can be.

Use a vase gourd, penguin gourd, or a gourd that is larger at the bottom while getting smaller at the top. It needs to be at least 9" tall and 5"–6" across. Cut off the top and clean out the gourd. You may want to sand the top rim. You can use a belt sander to sand the bottom of gourd so that it will stand up. I glue slices of wood to the bottom — it stands the gourd up and adds weight to the bottom, making it harder to knock over.

Spray-paint the inside with black spray paint. Paint the top of the rim with black acrylic paint. Put on latex gloves to keep your hands from getting stained. Dampen a paper towel with water and rub it over the entire gourd. Make sure it is damp but not wet. If it is too wet, wipe again with a dry paper towel.

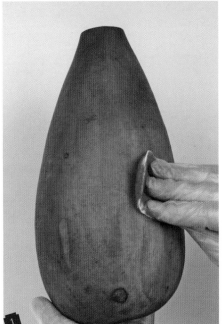

Apply turquoise leather dye to the entire gourd using a cotton round. Working on a tray, shake the leather dye. Add more dye if it starts to lighten while you are applying the dye. Apply a second coat if you feel it needs it.

Using the feathering method, pull purple leather dye down three-quarters of the gourd. I call this method "color feathering." Shake the purple leather dye. Apply it to your cotton round. Fold the cotton round in half. Starting at the top of the gourd, pull the cotton round down to about three-quarters of the gourd. Try to feather off the stroke. Do not leave spaces in between strokes. Apply until you have gone around the whole gourd.

Apply two more coats of purple leather dye and bring each layer up higher than the next. The purple leather dye will turn a green and gold color until you varnish it or heat-set it. Start at the top again and go halfway down the gourd. Complete this row around the gourd. Apply a third row of color, ending about a third from the top.

There is a YouTube video to help you with this process at: http://youtu.be/H-QqknYNmOc

Spray a light coat of varnish at this time to keep the dye from rubbing off as you continue to work. Keep it light. If you are using a dye that responds to heat set, you can use your embossing tool or heat gun to heat set the dye before using a light varnish spray. Do not use it again after you apply the wax.

Apply your design to the bottom half of the gourd. Allow room for the four longer strokes. Counting from the middle of the circle craft templates, take the first and second circles and place them one inside the other. Place them onto the gourd. Trace the inside of the smallest circle with your charcoal pencil. Remove that circle and trace the inside of the second circle.

Now, counting from the middle of the circle templates, take the fourth circle and position the smaller circles in the middle. Inside the ring, trace about an inch across the top, bottom, and both sides. This gives you your four points for the design. If you are not happy with your placement of the circles, remove the lines and try again. Place a dot in the middle of the circles with your charcoal pencil.

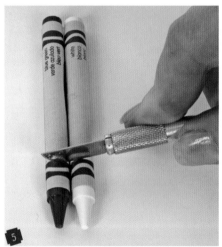

Cut your crayons just behind the double black lines for both white and blue-green to make turquoise. Set up your tray and plug in your melting pot. I used only one color in this design, but that color is made up of two crayons: half white and half blue-green. Both colors are found in the Crayola Crayons twenty-four pack.

With the tip pointed up, cut both crayons just below the bottom of the black lines. Put both pieces into the well to melt. Stir when completely melted until it becomes one solid color. Make sure that you add equal amounts of crayon to the well when it gets below three-quarters to keep the strokes similar in size.

Using the small end of Wax Design Tool #1, begin with the inside circle. Make sure you have warmed your tool. Start at the 12 o'clock position and pull the stroke to the middle. If you do not like it, take it off. Once you have completed that stroke, flip the gourd over so the bottom is on top. Pull the stroke again. Continue to divide your circle off until you have a total of sixteen strokes. If you need help, refer to the "Circle" section on page 20. Remove the charcoal pencil lines on the inside circle only. It is easier to remove it now rather than once a stroke has gone through it. This can be done with a damp Magic Eraser or cotton swab.

Switch out your Wax Design Tool to the #2 small end. Starting on the outside circle, pull a stroke in between each of the smaller strokes. Pull until you reach the center or until you run out of wax. Complete the circle. Make sure to add wax as needed to keep the well three-quarter to full at all times to keep the strokes consistent in size.

Pull a stroke from the top of the short outside line to the top of the inside circle. Change back to your Wax Design Tool #1 small end. Start at the top of short outside lines. Find the 12 o'clock stroke of the smaller circle. Line it up and pull the stroke until you run out of wax or reach the inside circle.

Place a stroke on each side of the stroke you just did. These strokes should be shorter than the center stroke. Do this to all four points.

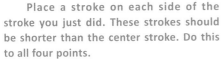

Going back to the Wax Design Tool #2 small end, apply dots in between the strokes on the outside circle. Even add dots in the section that the three strokes come into. Add dots to the top of the three strokes in the four points.

With your damp Magic Eraser, remove all the charcoal lines. You can use a damp Q-Tip also, if you have areas that are hard to get to. Dampen a paper towel and wipe over the design to get off the chalky film left by the Magic Eraser. Make sure you check the gourd in good light to see that all your lines have been removed before you varnish.

Apply at least two to three good coats of varnish. Refer back to the Varnishing chapter on page 30 if need be. Once the varnish is dry, you can embellish the gourd. With a piece of turquoise leather or suede lacing, glue it on the top of the rim. You can also tie it around the neck of the gourd if it is really long.

Tie your leather lacing around the top of the gourd. Hot glue your feathers on the leather. On this gourd, I used one peacock and two yellow and blue feathers. You can use a glue gun because the leather is absorbent. Make sure that one feather is longer than the other. Place the feathers so they can be seen when looking at the front of the gourd, but do not cover up any of the design.

Adding an embellishment. If you would like to glue an embellishment over or around the knot, do so at this time. Glue an embellishment to the center of the design using E6000. Set the gourd on its side to allow the embellishment to dry without sliding too much. Keep an eye on the embellishment for at least thirty minutes.

DESIGN TIP

Use larger circles for larger gourds and the mini circle templates for small gourds. This design can be used as a snowflake as well. To mix the design up, use different colors in the middle, for the outside circle, and for the dots. I would use the center color again for the three strokes in the four points. Just by changing the colors of the gourd and crayon, you can have a different gourd each time.

3 SETTING SUNS

SUPPLY LIST

Bottle gourd • light brown leather or ink dye • black acrylic paint • black spray paint • paintbrushes • low temp melting pot • Wax Design Tools #2, #1, and #0 • charcoal pencil • circle craft templates • Flex-e • Texture Brush and Insert • Crayola crayon colors dandelion, red, and brown • spray varnish • turquoise embellishments • E6000 • toothpicks • tray • hobby knife • paper towels • cotton balls and cotton rounds • latex gloves • water container • Mr. Clean Magic Eraser • hot glue gun • red and brown leather or suede lacing • scissors • craft foam • feather pattern • embossing foil • dry board

This design was inspired by the Navajo turquoise bracelet. There is a full circle in the middle and two half circles on either side. Use a bottle gourd at least 6" tall — the neck should go in so that you can tie a feather on later. The gourd needs to be at least 5" across. Cut and clean the gourd. Dye the gourd with a light brown. You can use a leather dye, ink dye, or alcohol ink. Starting at the middle of the circle templates, find the two smallest circles. Line them up in the middle, fat part of the gourd. Place the circles one inside the other.

Trace the two smallest circles on the gourd, one inside of the other. Draw a line across the middle. Put a dot where the line ends on each side of the circle. Trace the smallest circle with the charcoal pencil and remove the circle. Trace the inside of

the second circle. Draw a dot in the center of the circles. With a Flex-e, draw a line across the circles, dividing them in half. Place a dot where the line ends on each side of the circle.

Starting at the left, use the smaller circle template to line the circle up so that the dot is in the middle of the circle. Trace only the left of the circle. Repeat on the right side.

With dandelion, create the small circle in the middle. You should have your tray setup and your melting pots plugged in. Put the dandelion crayon into your melting pot. Dandelion is found in the box of twenty-four Crayola Crayons. Cut it just

above the word "Crayola." Break it into two pieces and put it into the well. Once it has melted, warm the small end of your Wax Design Tool #1. Doing the center circle first, start at the top and pull the stroke to the center dot. Flip the gourd over and pull the stroke again. Keep dividing your circle off until you have a total of sixteen strokes. Refer back to the section on Circle design on page 20 if need be.

Still working with the dandelion crayon, switch to the small end of Wax Design Tool #2. Warm the tool. Starting with the circle to the left, pull a stroke from the middle of the half circle to the dot or until you run out of wax. Pull a stroke just on the

outside of the double circles on the half circles to the dot. Do this on the other side of the half circle.

Divide the half circles in between the strokes on each side.

Put two strokes in between each of the strokes on the half circle. This will complete your half circle. Complete the other half circle on the other side of the design.

Pull red strokes from the outside circle in between the smaller inside strokes. If you are working with one melting pot, clean out the dandelion and put red Crayola into your melting pot. Still using the small end of Wax Design Tool #2, pull strokes from the outside circle to the center or until your wax runs out. Complete the circle.

With your damp Magic Eraser, remove all the charcoal lines. You can also use a damp Q-Tip if you have areas that are hard to reach. Dampen a paper towel and wipe over the design to get the chalky film off left by the Magic Eraser. Check under good light to see that all your lines have been removed before you varnish.

With brown, add dots between the red strokes. Add dots above the dandelion strokes on the half circles. Clean out your melting pot if you are working with only one. Add brown Crayola to the melting pot. Still using the small end of Wax Design Tool #2, add dots between the red strokes above the dandelion strokes. Switch to the small end of Wax Design Tool #1 and add dots above the dandelion strokes in the half circle designs. Make sure that the dots are above and not on the dandelion strokes.

Melt dandelion crayon across the insert. Clean your melting pot out and lay your metal insert on top of the metal part of the well. Make sure the lip is facing up. Refer to the section about Texture Brush and Insert on page 9. Allow the insert to get warm.

Always start with your lighter color. Take your dandelion crayon and melt the crayon across the top of the insert until it has a nice layer. You do not want too much crayon because then it will create a heavier texture.

Pounce dandelion texture onto your gourd. Do not go over your design. Take your clean Texture Brush, pounce it into the wax, and then pounce it onto the gourd. You will only get a couple of pounces because the wax is cooling. Do not put any on your design. Apply texture to the rest of the gourd. Remember that you are going to apply another color of wax.

Pounce some brown texture onto your gourd. Do not do too much. Once you have applied the dandelion texture to the gourd, clean out the insert and brush with your paper towel. You are melting the wax out of the brush. Melt and wipe onto the paper towel and clean the insert, repeating until you have removed enough of the wax to go to the darker color. Since you are using the darker color, the entire dandelion color needs to be removed from the brush. With a clean insert, melt the brown on the insert. Pounce the brown onto the gourd, applying texture to the entire gourd except for the design. Apply the brown a little lighter than the dandelion. Do not muddy it. If you get a larger chunk of wax, remove it with your hobby knife. Varnish the gourd at this time. Refer back to the chapter on Varnishing, on page 30, if need be.

A FEATHER EMBELLISHMENT

To make the feather, you are going to use 36- to 40-gauge metal sheets. It is also called embossing foil or aluminum tooling foil and can be found in hobby stores in a roll or a sheet. I like the 36-gauge foil. It is heavier and holds the shape better. Foil also comes in several colors.

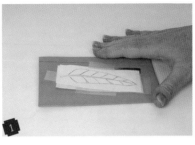

Make a copy of your original feather pattern so that you always have one. Cut a piece of the foil the size of your pattern. Take the pattern and the metal sheet and tape it onto the craft foam. Tape it to at least two sides. You have to have the craft foam to make this work. If you don't, you will have a flat piece of metal. It allows the pressure of tracing the lines to sink into the foam and makes the ridges.

Trace the entire pattern. Using the small end of Wax Design Tool #2, trace all of the lines on the feather pattern. Push fairly hard with the Wax Design Tool. This makes a deep impression on the metal. If you push too lightly, you will not have nice lines on your feather. Start with the line down the middle. Now, trace around the outside of the feather and then do the middle veins.

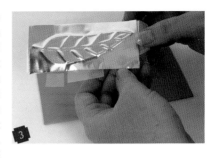

Remove the pattern and turn the foil over. Make sure that you have traced all the lines. You can lift the pattern to see if you missed any. If you need to trace some that you missed, make sure that you realign the pattern. Remove the pattern and flip the feather over to the other side. The raised area of the feather should be up. Make sure to keep it on the craft foam.

Trace the smaller feather veins between each section. Switch to the large end of Wax Design Tool #0. You are going to go in between the big vein lines with a bunch of little lines. Add as many little lines to each section as possible. Do not go over the part that you previously raised. Do the entire feather. Keep the lines going in the same direction as the veins you did earlier.

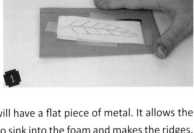

Using little craft scissors, cut around the outside of the feather. See where the line on the edge has gone flat? Cut along that flat edge. If you cut on the raised line, you will lose the curve of that line.

Leave a long stem at the top of the feather. This will make attaching it to the gourd easier. You can use that stem to glue it onto the leather, tie it onto the gourd, or bend it over the edge of a bowl.

Cut the little pie sections out of the feather. I recommend three to four on each feather. It helps give the feather an airy look. Feathers are not solid. Do not cut them too far in — it will weaken your feather. Make sure you remove some of the metal;

do not just cut a line. Where you have trimmed out your little pie sections of the feather, lightly round the corners. The metal is very sharp, so please be careful!

Flip your feather over again so that the deep lines (first side) are down. Retrace the pattern lines again with the Wax Design Tool #2. Some of your shape was lost when cutting it out. Also, by tracing your lines again, you add more of a curve to your feather. Do not overdo it, though. You have your highs and lows and by working it back and forth more, you even it out. Keep it simple. I believe in this case less is better.

Wrap the leather lacing around your gourd twice. Hot glue your feather onto the leather. To put your feather onto the gourd, use leather or suede lacing. Wrap the leather lacing around the gourd twice and do one single knot. Take the feather and hot glue the stem onto the knot. Make sure you have it high enough so you can tie another knot over the top to hold it in place. Bend the feather to the shape of the gourd. Most

feathers are not just straight. I like to have them highlight the pattern on my gourd. See what size feather and what direction you want it to go on your gourd before you make it. You can also leave it straight. Try adding a couple of feathers on a gourd.

There is a YouTube video to help you with this process at:
http://youtu.be/kdZzOkMvr54

Glue on embellishments with E6000. Hot glue a turquoise stone or another color stone on top of the knot to help cover it up. Put an embellishment in the center of the big circles and in the center of the two half circles where the dots were. Make sure the color embellishments you choose make your design pop.

DESIGN TIP

You have completed the second project. Remember that you can simply change the base colors and the crayons to create a new gourd each time. Draw your own feathers. Do not make it hard. Keep them simple. Make them different shapes and sizes, and curve them to frame your artwork. I love using them with the wax design. Think of more than feathers. You can make leaves, horses, cactus — the list keeps going. What do you like? Apply what you learned to something new.

MIDNIGHT STAR

SUPPLY LIST

Gourd • black acrylic paint • black spray paint • paintbrushes • low temp melting pot • Wax Design Tools #2 and #1 • charcoal pencil • circle craft templates • Flex-e • white Crayola • spray varnish • black embellishments • E6000 • toothpicks • tray • hobby knife • paper towels • cotton balls and cotton rounds • latex gloves • water container • Mr. Clean Magic Eraser • dry board

Start with a round gourd at least 7" tall and 8" across. Counting from the middle of the circle templates, find the fourth ring — use this ring for the template to cut the top of the gourd. Clean out the inside and spray-paint it black. Using black acrylic paint, basecoat the rim and the rest of the gourd. You will need at least two coats of black paint. Make sure the first layer is dry before you start the second layer. Spray varnish the gourd one time. This keeps the black gourd clean.

There is a YouTube video to help you with this process at:
http://youtu.be/LC1r7l3qTpM

Divide your gourd into three sections. Put a dot in the middle of each section. Using the Flex-e, measure the middle of the gourd. Take that number and divide it by three. Mark three dots onto the gourd with your charcoal pencil. To make sure that your three dots are in the middle, measure from the top of the gourd to the bottom and divide that in half. Adjust your three dots on the gourd if needed.

With the dot in the middle, trace the two smallest circles onto each section. Counting from the middle of the circle templates, find the first and second rings. Set them one inside the other. Place the dots in the center of the circles. Trace the inside of the smallest circle with the charcoal pencil and then remove the smallest circle. Trace the inside of the next circle.

Create the inside circle. Do in all three sections. Set up your tray and plug in your melting pot. You will only need one melting pot and one crayon for this project. Fill up the well with the white crayon. White needs stirring a little more than other crayons. If  you notice that the color has started to separate from the wax, you need to stir it. If the white drips more than usual, check the air flow around you. If it continues, take a cotton ball and absorb a little of the white crayon out of the melting pot. If you have a drop or want to remove a stroke, remove the stroke with your hobby knife the best you can. You will touch up the black paint at the end of our project. Using the small end of Wax Design Tool #1, start with the smallest circle. Pull the wax to the center. You should have sixteen strokes to complete the small circle. Repeat on the other two circles.

Create the outside circle pulling each stroke between each of the smaller strokes. Do all three sections. Switch to the small end of Wax Design Tool #2. Starting on the outside of the larger circle, pull your strokes in between the  strokes of the smaller circle. Complete the circle. Repeat on the other two circles.

Pull a long stroke out above the small strokes. Work clockwise until you complete the circle. Do all three sections. Now, pull strokes out, starting between the larger strokes just above the smaller circle. Pull the stroke until the wax runs out. This will keep the strokes close to the same length. Repeat on the other two circles. Add wax to your well when it gets below three-quarters full.

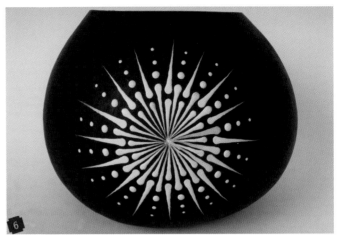

Starting just above the second circle, do three descending dots, going outward. Do all three sections. Still using the small end of Wax Design Tool #2, add descending dots. Start just above the second circle and do three descending dots — these should get smaller as they move toward the outside of the gourd. Repeat on the other two circles.

Find the middle between the circles and mark a dot with your charcoal pencil. You should have a total of three dots.

Place a dot and two strokes pulled out, another dot and two strokes pulled out and one more dot and two more strokes followed by a descending dot. Using the charcoal pencil, mark two strokes going up away from the dot. Mark a dot and mark two more strokes above the dot. Mark one more dot and two more strokes above that dot. Mark three descending dots at the top. Repeat on the other two circles. Start at the middle dot and mark two strokes going down away from the dot. Mark a dot and mark two more strokes below that dot. Mark one more dot and two more strokes below that dot. Mark three descending dots, going toward the bottom of the gourd. Repeat on the other two circles. Still using the small end of Wax Design Tool #2, put a wax dot where you marked it with the charcoal pencil. On the top strokes, pull them up until they run out of wax.

41

Turn your gourd over and repeat the design again. Do all three sections. Pull the bottom strokes down until they run out of wax. Complete the design by adding three descending dots to the top and bottom of the design and across the middle where the design meets.

NOTE: If you can only get two sets of strokes and dots on each side of the middle dot, that is okay. Remember that this is just an idea — take what you have learned and apply it your way or adjust the pattern to fit your gourd. Now, with your damp Magic Eraser, remove all the charcoal pencil lines. Wipe again with a damp paper towel to remove the chalky film left by the Magic Eraser.

Touch up any mistakes with your base color. Using the black acrylic paint you used for your basecoat, touch up any areas that are dirty or were messed up when you were taking off the wax. If you have any white flecks near your dots or on the gourd, you can paint them or remove them with your hobby knife. The paint will appear flat because you varnished the other layer of black paint. That is okay. It will blend in as soon as you varnish it again.

Varnish your gourd and glue on embellishments. Make sure that you check to see that you have removed all your lines. Varnish the gourd. Refer to the chapter on Varnishing, page 30, if need be. Once the varnish is dry, you can glue your embellishments on in the center of the three circle designs. Use E6000 to glue them on. Watch the embellishments for at least thirty minutes to make sure they do not slide. It is harder to watch embellishments when you have them on all sides. Make sure you are watching all three sections or glue them on one at a time and allow drying time for each one.

SOUTHWEST DRAGONFLY

SUPPLY LIST

Gourd • red or bright red leather or ink dye • black spray paint • low temp melting pot • Wax Design Tools #2, #1 and #0 • charcoal pencil • craft circle templates • Flex-e • Crayola Crayon colors blue-green, dandelion, brown, and white • pumpkin, black, and barn red acrylic paints • paintbrush • spray varnish • sea sponge • paper pallet or paper plate • embellishments • E6000 • toothpicks • tray • hobby knife • paper towels • cotton balls and cotton rounds • latex gloves • water container • Mr. Clean Magic Eraser • dry board

Start with a canteen gourd that is at least 5" tall and 9" across. The height and width are very important to get all of this design onto the gourd. Starting from the middle of the circle templates, find the fourth ring. Place this on top of the gourd and trace it as close to the center of the top as possible. Use that circle to cut off the top of the gourd. The size of the circle is very important because of the measurements used for the rim decoration. Clean out the inside of the gourd and spray-paint it black. Paint the rim with black acrylic paint. Using a red or bright red ink dye, leather dye, or alcohol ink dye, stain the gourd.

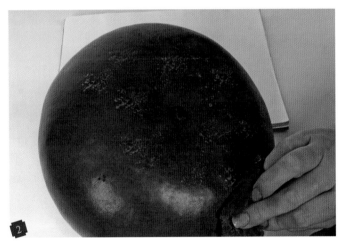

Pull your paint out and then pounce into the color with your sea sponge to get a nice even design. You are going to sponge over the dye. The correct way to sponge-paint is to take a damp sea sponge and wring all of the water out of it. Make sure that it

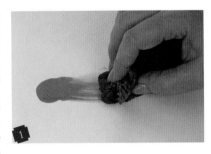

does not drip. Put pumpkin or orange acrylic paint onto a paper pallet or a paper plate. Do not put your sponge in the middle of the paint. This will just give you a glob of paint when sponging. Take your sponge and pull the paint across the paper and pounce into the paint with your sponge.

Pounce color all over your gourd. Leave spaces in between your pouncing. Once you have loaded the sponge, pounce it onto the gourd. I start on the bottom of my gourd so that I can see if the paint is too dark. Load again when the paint starts to get lighter. Leave spaces for the darker color. You should always start with the light color first. Sometimes the pumpkin color will not show until you have varnished the gourd, so do not worry if you are not seeing too much color. When you are satisfied with your sponging, rinse the sponge and wring it until it has no water dripping out.

There is a YouTube video to help you with this process at:
http://youtu.be/VyCw0z6sPl8

Come back with your darker color and pounce in between the last color. Using a dark red or a barn red acrylic paint, sponge this color onto the gourd. Pounce the color off and start at the bottom to make sure the color is not too dark. Apply to the rest of

the gourd. Do not add too much, as you can always add more later.

Directly across the rim, trace three-quarters of the circle on again. Trace on the inside of the ring. Go across to the other side of the rim. Line up the charcoal lines with the rim. Your charcoal mark should be in the center of the ring directly across from the other circle.

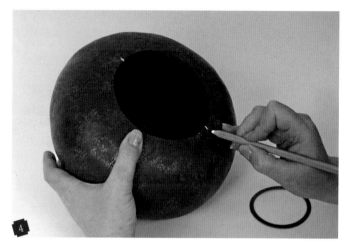

Using your charcoal pencil, divide the rim in half and mark it on both sides. This helps to align the circles for the rim design.

Two more should fit on each side of the rim for a total of six. Two half circles will fit in between each of the ones you have done. Line them up and see how they fit. It is okay to have a little space in between the half circles. Trace on the inside of the half circles. Repeat on the other side. Put a dot in the center of each half circle right next to the rim.

Using the mini circle templates, you are going to trace three-quarters of the circle onto the rim. For this project, you will be using the mini circle templates. This allows you a bigger variety of smaller circles. Counting from the middle, find the fifth ring and lay it on the rim of the gourd with the charcoal mark in the middle. Leave about three-quarters of the ring on the gourd. Mark on the ring with your charcoal pencil to know where to line it up for the next circle.

Add six more circles to the middle of the gourd. The circles should line up in between the circles on the rim. Using the same circle, in the middle of the gourd, line up the middle of the circle to where the circles come together at the top on the rim. Trace on the

inside of the circle. Repeat for a total of six circles. Three of these circles are for placement of the dragonfly only. Make sure that you leave enough room for the design and do not end up running into the rim design.

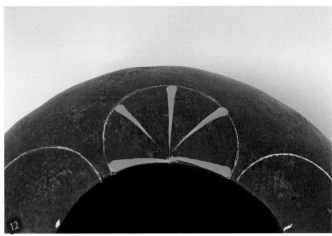

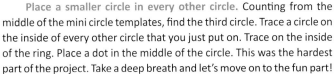

Place a smaller circle in every other circle. Counting from the middle of the mini circle templates, find the third circle. Trace a circle on the inside of every other circle that you just put on. Trace on the inside of the ring. Place a dot in the middle of the circle. This was the hardest part of the project. Take a deep breath and let's move on to the fun part!

Pull a stroke in between the middle stroke and the one on the left. Pull a stroke in between the stroke in the middle and the one on the right. Repeat in the other five half circles on the rim.

To make turquoise color, use half white and half blue-green crayon. Set up your tray. You are going to be using three colors. Plug in your melting pots. The first color is going to be a mixture of half white and half blue-green found in the twenty-four box of Crayola Crayons. This makes the wonderful turquoise color. With the tip pointed up, cut both crayons just below the bottom of the black lines. Put both pieces into the well to melt. Stir when completely melted until it becomes one solid color. Make sure that you add equal amounts of crayon to the well when it gets below three-quarters to keep the strokes similar in size.

Add two strokes in between each of the strokes completed. There are four sets of two strokes in each half circle. Repeat in the other five half circles on the rim.

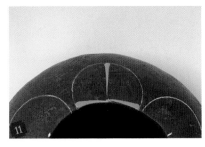

Pull the first stroke down the middle to the dot at the edge of the rim. Pull a stroke from the left and right to the dot. Start with the rim, using the small end of Wax Design Tool #2. Turn the gourd so that you are working with the circle across from you. Pull the first stroke down the center of the half circle until you get to the dot or run out of wax. Pull the second stroke to the left of the half circle, following the rim, until you reach the dot. Pull the next stroke from the right of the half circle, following the rim, until you reach the dot. Repeat in the other five half circles on the rim.

In the single circles, make a mark about one-third from the top of the circle. Still using the small end of Wax Design Tool #2 and starting on the outside of the circle just above the dot on the right side, pull a stroke to the dot. Drop down below the dot, still on the outside of the right side of the circle, and pull another stroke to the dot. Repeat on the other side of the circle. You are creating wings for your dragonfly.

Complete the three small circles in the larger circles on the side of your gourd. Switch to the large end of Wax Design Tool #0. Pull strokes until you get to the dot in the middle. You will have a total of sixteen strokes.

Pull strokes in from the second circle in between each of the smaller strokes. Place the dandelion crayon into one of the melting pots. Switch to the small end of Wax Design Tool #2. Starting at the second set of circles, pull color in between all of the turquoise strokes. Complete all three circles.

Above the smaller strokes pull strokes out from the circle. Place the brown crayon into your last melting pot. You are still using the small end of Wax Design Tool #2. Starting at the double circles, just above the turquoise strokes and between the dandelion strokes, pull a brown stroke out away from the circle until you run out of wax. Do this above each turquoise stroke in the circle. Complete all three circles.

Starting at the top of the circle, pull a large stroke connecting wings to dragonfly. Add a dot for the head and two antennas. Switch to the large end of Wax Design Tool #2. Allow tool to warm in the melting pot. Pull a stroke to where the two turquoise strokes meet to form the dragonfly body. Start at the top of the circle and pull the stroke slowly toward the bottom. Remember, the slower you pull the stroke, the further it goes. Dot a head if you feel it needs one. Now, switch to the small end of Wax Design Tool #0. Pull two antenna strokes to meet the head, one on each side of the head of the dragonfly.

On the rim, in between the top half circles, draw a line with your charcoal pencil. The line should start where the half circles start on either side of the line. Mark all six places on the rim.

Pull the stroke toward the middle. Do a smaller stroke on each side of the middle stroke. Pull the brown strokes on the marked line on the rim with the small end of Wax Design Tool #1. Pull the stroke until you reach the rim or a stroke if the strokes are close together. Pull a shorter stroke to the left of the first stroke and then a shorter stroke to the right of the first stroke.

Still using the small end of Wax Design Tool #1, add a dandelion dot above the longer brown stroke. Do this on all six strokes around the rim.

Now, add dandelion dots in between each of the turquoise strokes on the rim. You can switch to the small end of Wax Design Tool #1 if you find that the dots are too big and you do not have enough room.

Using the small end of Wax Design Tool #2, you can do descending dots in between the wings of the dragonfly to add some more color and movement to them.

In the double circles above the dandelion strokes, add turquoise descending dots. Going back to the turquoise color, make sure the well is full. Using the small end of Wax Design Tool #2, add three descending dots in the

double circles above the dandelion strokes. The dots start next to the stroke and go away from the circle. Do this all the way around the circle. Complete all three circles.

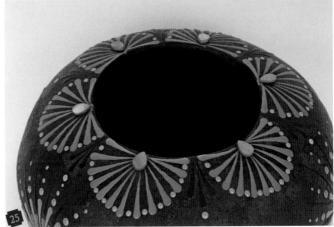

Gluing your embellishments. With your damp Magic Eraser, remove all the charcoal pencil lines. Wipe again with a damp paper towel to remove the chalky film left by the Magic Eraser. Varnish the gourd. (Refer to the chapter on Varnishing, on page 30, if need be). I used nine embellishments on this gourd: six for the top and three for the double circles. Once the varnish is dry, you can glue on the embellishments. The six on top are easier to glue on because the surface is flatter. Remember to put the glue on the embellishment and not the gourd. Remove all of the glue strings before you apply the embellishment to the gourd. This keeps the strings off of the gourd.

Watch the three embellishments that you glued in the double circles. The embellishments may slide for the first thirty minutes. It helps to place them onto the gourd and hold them in place for a couple of minutes. Keep checking them. Be sure to look on all sides of the gourd.

I love to work on canteen gourds when doing rim work. You can see all of the rim's design when looking at the gourd, and it changes the focus of the design from the sides to the top of the gourd. You can create beautiful gourds by just doing the rim. Think of other techniques to add to the sides and just do the top with the wax. You could also build on the scallops at the top. Keep adding layers of scallops all the way down the gourd.

EYE OF THE DIAMOND

SUPPLY LIST

Gourd • mahogany leather dye • back spray paint • black acrylic paint • paintbrush • low temp melting pot • Wax Design Tools #2 and #0 • charcoal pencil • square templates • Crayola Crayon colors blue-green, white, dandelion, and black • spray varnish • embellishments • hot glue gun • E6000 • toothpicks • tray • hobby knife • paper towels • cotton balls and cotton rounds • latex gloves • water container • Mr. Clean Magic Eraser • turquoise leather or suede strip • feathers • dry board

Enough of the circle designs — let's get into a design using the squares. Start with a Chinese bottle gourd or a vase gourd at least 12" tall and 7" across. Cut off the top and clean out the inside. Spray the inside of the gourd with black spray paint and paint the rim with black acrylic paint. Dye the gourd with mahogany leather dye.

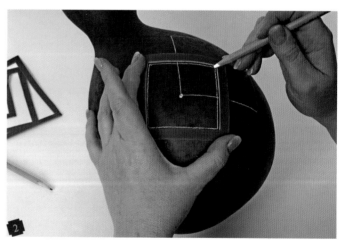

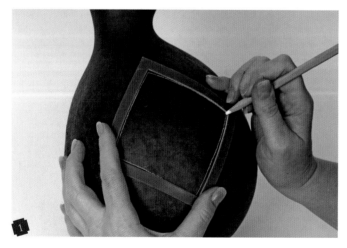

Trace the large square in the middle of your gourd. Place a dot on the two side corners. You will be using the square templates this time. Starting from the inside of the squares, find the fourth square. Trace it in the middle of the gourd, using a charcoal pencil. Make sure that you leave enough room at the top and bottom of the square for all of the design. Trace on the inside of the square. Make a dot at the left and right corners of your square.

Trace the smaller square on the left, with the dot in the middle of the square. Counting from the middle of the template, find the third square and place it to the left of your larger square. Line it up so that the dot you did on the left will be in the center of this square. This will form a smaller square where the two squares meet. Trace on the inside of the square with the charcoal pencil. Repeat on the other side.

Using your charcoal pencil, mark a line across the center of the big square, meeting the two little squares on each side.

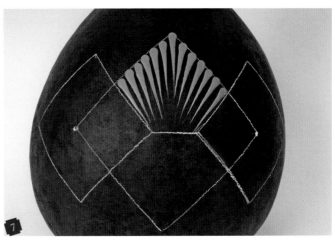

Add two strokes in between each of the strokes you did on both the left and the right — this will complete the top section of the square.

Pull a stroke from the top of the middle square toward the line. Just above the left square, pull a stroke to the line. Repeat on the right side. Set up your tray and plug in your melting pots. You will be using three colors for this project. You will be mixing the first color to create the turquoise. Mix the white and blue-green half and half. Add both pieces to the well. Mix when the colors have melted. Using the small end of Wax Design Tool #2 and starting with the largest square on the top part of the pattern, pull a stroke from the center toward the line. You most likely will run out of wax. Pull the next stroke just outside the little square on your left. Follow the line until you reach the center line. Pull the next stroke just outside the little square on your right. Follow the line until you reach the center line.

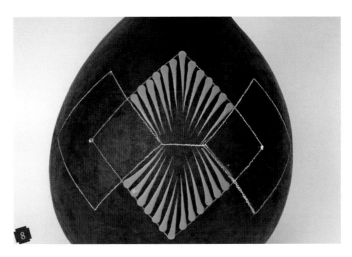

Flip the gourd over and repeat all the steps on the bottom section of the square.

On the left side of the square, put a stroke in between the two strokes that you just did. On the right side of the square, put a stroke in between the top stroke and the one above the little square.

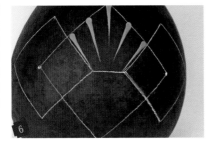

Still using the small end of Wax Design Tool #2, go to the left square. Pull a stroke from all three points of the square to the center dot. Do not worry if the stroke does not make it to the center — pull until the wax runs out. Repeat this process on the right side.

49

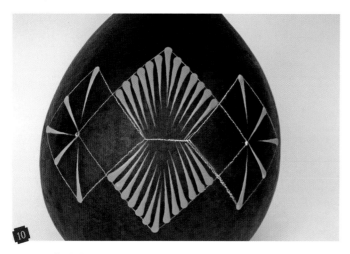

On the left square, add a stroke in the middle of the strokes that you just completed. Repeat on the right side.

On the left square, pull a stroke just outside the little square on the top half until you reach the center dot. Pull a stroke just outside the little square on the bottom half until you reach the center dot. Repeat both these steps on the right side. Add more crayon if the wax starts to get low in the well.

Go back in between each of the strokes you made in the left-side square and add a stroke in the middle of those areas. Repeat this on the right-side square.

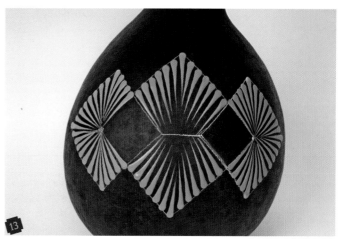

Starting with the left square, add one more stroke in between all of the strokes that you just completed. It will seem tight, but there should be enough room. This is what gives the design great texture. Now repeat on the right side.

Pull three dandelion strokes out from the points of the middle squares and three strokes out on the sides. Put the dandelion crayon into the well. Still using the small end of Wax Design #2, pull a stroke out from the points of the middle square. These  strokes should line up with the turquoise strokes. Allow room between the turquoise and dandelion strokes. You do not want them to touch. Pull the stroke until it runs out of wax. Pull a stroke to the right of the first stroke and to the left of the first stroke. Repeat on the bottom of the square and in both the right and left side squares.

Pull dandelion strokes out from where the square meets just above the little squares. Pull three strokes out on the top left and three strokes out on the top right. Move to the bottom of the gourd, just below the little square, and pull three strokes out on the left and three strokes out on the right.

little squares with your charcoal pencil. Starting with the square on the left, pull a stroke from all four corners to the dot in the center. Add a stroke in between each of the four strokes for a total of eight. If you have room to add a stroke in between each of the other strokes, do so at this time. Repeat this process on the right side.

Still using Wax Design Tool #0, apply a dot of the dandelion to the center of the black squares. Make this a quick dot as you do not want the tool to melt the black wax underneath. You could also add a small embellishment here instead of a dot. Remove all of your charcoal lines. Varnish the gourd and let it dry.

Put black dots at the ends of the dandelion strokes. Put the black crayon into the melting pot. Staying with the Wax Design Tool #2, add dots to the top tails of the dandelion strokes. The dots should make a point. You are cleaning up the stroke tails. On the two middle dandelion strokes and the two side strokes, the dots should form a point going out. On the other strokes, the dots should form a point going in.

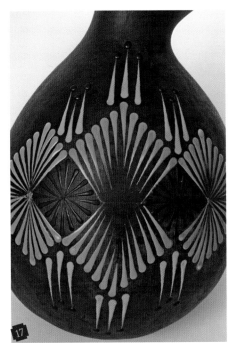

With Black, create two little squares in the middle of the design. Now switch to the large end of Wax Design Tool #0. Make sure you warm your tool. Make a dot in the center of the

Wrap a leather or suede lacing around the gourd two times. Tie a knot — make sure the knot is to the side of the gourd; it should accentuate your design, but not cover any of it. Put hot glue on the leather knot and place your feathers on top. You should use two or three feathers and they should be descending down the side of the gourd. Once you have glued the feathers on, tie a knot over the top of the feathers. You could hot glue a stone over the knot if you wanted. ***Warning: If your varnish is not dry, your feathers will stick to it.***

Glue your embellishments on with E6000. I used a larger stone in the middle and two smaller ones in the center of the outside designs. The bigger the stone, the more you need to watch the stone. The stone will slide until the glue is set. Since you are working with only one side of the gourd, lay it down to help keep the stone from sliding.

DESIGN TIP

Change the colors to create a new look for this design. Add more strokes, pulling away from the gourd, or do less. Instead of strokes, use descending dots. Put two squares together instead of three. Add two smaller squares to the sides to wrap around the gourd. Do designs on both sides and add another square to join them. The design possibilities are limitless. I have tried to get you thinking about what you can design. Change out the real feathers and use the foil feather you learned how to make (see page 38). I am here to inspire you. You can do this. You can create your own wonderful designs, while having lots of fun!

DROPS

Drops are just part of the technique, but you should be able to keep them to a minimum. I can do a design without one drop. The lighter the color, the thinner the wax is and the easier it will drop. Test your colors with the tool you want to use before you try it on your design. If the color that is dripping has been sitting in the melting pot for awhile, stir it really well to cool it down a little. If your tool has been sitting in the wax or chimney, pick it up and wipe it clean very well with the paper towel. This will also help cool the wax down. Make sure that your well is not too full. You should be able to see the rectangle in the well. If it is still dripping, take a cotton ball and absorb a little wax out of the well.

Make sure that after pulling the tool out of the wax you slow down. Do not be in a hurry to reach the gourd. Moving your hand too fast can also make the wax drip. The wax will not cool off that fast. Work at a normal pace. When you have completed part of your design, take the tool around the design to the area you are working on, not across the design. This way, if you happen to have a drop, it does not fall on your design. Turn the gourd. The shorter the distance between the gourd and the melting pot, the less likely it is to drip. Do not have your melting pot more than 12" from the gourd, and be careful not to have the gourd a

long way from the melting pot by, for example, setting it down in your lap. If you are still getting drops, make sure there is no breeze. If you are still getting drops, switch to a smaller tool, which picks up less wax and will not drip as much. You can also change to a thicker color.

If a drop has fallen on part of your design, allow it to dry and then take your hobby knife and cut around the stroke it fell on.

Remove the cut part of the drop.

Since this is two layers of wax, a lot of the time you can remove the top layer of the wax since the bottom wax layer was already dry when the drop occurred. Take your hobby knife and gently scrape off the top layer. The worst that will happen is that you have to take the stroke off and put it on again.

*There is a YouTube video to help you with this process at: **http://youtu.be/uBd-UVS5IR4***

KEEP THE GOURD FLAT

Try to keep the area of the gourd that you are working on as flat as possible. If you put a stroke on and the gourd is slanting down, the stroke is going to try to run away from you. It is working with gravity. It is the same for dots. Allow them to dry a couple of seconds before moving the gourd.

*There is a YouTube video to help you with this process at: **http://youtu.be/wz4efnmxLEo***

TROUBLESHOOTING ABOUT STROKES

What it looks like when you go over a stroke. The wax cools so fast that you cannot go over a stroke. It is natural that you want to fix it. If you try to go over the stroke, it will just make a mess. Wait for the wax to dry and remove it with your hobby knife. Put the stroke on again.

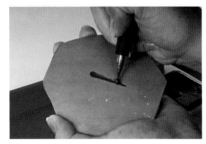

*There is a YouTube video to help you with this process at: **http://youtu.be/PH8tSEQYBJ0***

Putting strokes too close together while the strokes are still warm makes the strokes run together. When applying strokes right next to each other, make sure that the first stroke has cooled. If the wax is still warm on both strokes, the wax will run together. The warm wax seems to attract the other warm wax and draws it in. When I am working with strokes that are in close proximity of each other, I will do every other one and come back in and put the strokes in after the ones around it have cooled. This is also true for dots. When doing a bunch of random dots, I dot the first layer not touching. Allow it to cool and then come back in with the second set of dots.

*There is a YouTube video to help you with this process at: **http://youtu.be/LtkSii_TxF4***

You can cross over the bottom of a stroke where the wax is thinner. Wax cools so fast that you should not apply warm wax over cold wax. This keeps you from crossing over the wide part of a stroke, but since the tail is so thin you can pull a stroke across the

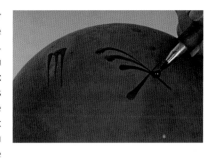

bottom half of a stroke. You can also come up next to a stroke and pull the tails together, allowing you to do design like a fleur-de-lis.

DESIGN TIP

Swirl designs are really popular right now and are great when working with this wax technique. You are only limited by how far you can pull your stroke. Look at all the designs around you. You will see them in shirts, purses, pillows, bedspreads — the list goes on and on. Paisleys are another great design. Between the strokes and dots, the possibilities are limitless.

CONSISTENCY OF THE SIZE OF THE STROKES

The trick to keeping your strokes the same size is to make sure that you load your tool in the wax in the same spot and the same way each time you dip into the well. Make sure that you pull the tool out fast, since pulling the tool out too slowly removes the wax. If you get nervous and go up and down in the well, you are removing wax. Watch your hand when you are learning. You might not realize that you are doing this. Pull the wax tool straight up and out — not at an angle. Make sure that the well is full. Your strokes will start to get smaller when there is less wax in the well. Do not let your well get less than three-quarters full.

If you need a smaller stroke for just a couple of times, load your Wax Design Tool in the back corner of the well. This will remove some of the wax. Test the stroke: if it is still too large, dip it in the corner of the well, but only go half way down into the wax. This

method should only be used for a couple of strokes. It will not keep the strokes consistent. You should try to use a smaller tool. This is only for one or two strokes where you do not have a smaller tool available.

There is a YouTube video to help you with this process at:
http://youtu.be/-7Cwfq8RuVY

If the tails of the strokes are broken or skip, you are pulling the stroke too fast. By pulling the stroke too fast, you are not allowing the wax time to apply to the gourd. Slow down. Pull the stroke nice and slow.

You can repair a stroke or dot on a design even if you have varnished it. Take your hobby knife and remove the broken strokes or dots. With the hobby knife, remove the varnish around the stroke. Put your stroke or dots back on and varnish the gourd again.

There is a YouTube video to help you with this process at:
http://youtu.be/VaTK1Z11xZU

WAX MELTING TIPS AND PRECAUTIONS

MELTING THE WAX FOR A DIFFERENT LOOK

You can create a different look by melting the wax after you have applied it to the gourd. If you want a '60s look or a Fourth of July fireworks show on your gourd, you can melt the wax a little. Take a blow dryer or a heat tool. Apply the heat to a section at a time. Hold heat over the wax until it melts just a little. If you want it to run more, then apply more heat. Let that section cool and start on the next section.

You can also glue crayons onto your gourd with a hot glue gun. Once they are glued in place, use a blow dryer or heat gun to melt the bottom half of the crayon. Follow the wax down to melt it more. This creates a colorful and fun gourd, and is very visually rewarding.

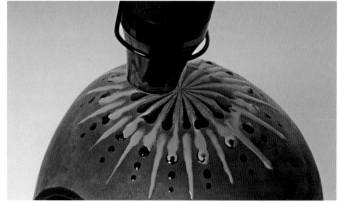

Melting your wax can be done with a heat tool.

Gourd design showing wax that was melted with a heat tool for a different effect.

Heating your wax makes great Fourth of July gourds. Melting some designs more than others makes it look like stages of fireworks.

KEEP OUT OF DIRECT SUNLIGHT

Like all artwork, especially gourd art, you should not put the gourd in direct sunlight. Sunlight will fade colors. If you are traveling in the car with the gourd, make sure that you have already varnished it and keep it in an area where it is out of the direct sunlight. Varnishing changes the melting point of the wax on the gourd, so do not travel with a gourd that you have not varnished. I travel with mine in an insulated bag. For jewelry or smaller items, apply thick layers of lacquer or glaze so that none of the wax is exposed and cannot melt. Refer back to the chapter on Varnishing on page 30 if need be.

Melted crayons that were glued onto the gourd then melted half way.

APPLYING CRAYOLA CRAYONS TO OTHER PROJECTS

The wax (Crayola Crayons) can be applied to lots of other things as well. You can apply it to rocks. Spray-varnish the rock first so that it is not absorbent. Put your wax design onto the rock and varnish again. You can also apply it to wood. If the wood is porous, varnish it first. You can tell if you need to varnish first by pulling a stroke across that item. If it pulls well, you are good to go. If the stroke is broken and it is hard to pull, remove the stroke, varnish, and start again. Varnish again when you are done with the design.

Gourd glued on a slice of wood with the Wax Design added to both.

Wax Design on a piece of wood.

Create your own picture on a canvas. You can paint the canvas with acrylic paints if you would like and then apply a pattern on with wax.

You can even put the wax on glass or metal. You would need to put a heavy lacquer or glaze over it to keep the wax on. I like to use the glass floral stones during the holidays to make little designs that I can pass out to let people know they are special. It will make their day.

Wax applied to canvas.

The wax can be applied to plastic and glass when varnished correctly.

Put a wax design on clay pots, party or holiday decorations, and craft items, such as fun foam. The list goes on and on. The only items this technique will not work well on are ones that are too absorbent, such as felt.

Cards made out of copies of designs.

You can also use this technique on paper. I do all my design work on paper first. The thinner the paper, the more the paper can bend. When you bend a stroke, it will pop off the paper, so if you want to do a design that you can keep, put it on a thick cardstock or cardboard and frame it. You can also make a color copy of the design and use that for cards or pictures. Using this method you can make great cards and gift tags for various occasions, including birthdays and Christmas.

These fun projects were all created with the help of wax. There is a "free" YouTube video for each project shown and much, much more.

Take all of these ideas and build on them. I created this book so that you can create something beautiful without having to spend a lot of time and money on it. I believe that everyone can create something wonderful. This method is not hard and can be mastered with very little practice. Take your creations to the next level. Try something you like or a design you put together. My job is to introduce the method and start the thinking process.

For more ideas, visit my YouTube site at **http://www.youtube. com/user/Miriamjoy123?feature=mhee** or my Facebook page at "Miriam Joy Gourd Creations."

ORIENTAL JAR. Radiant Rain®
background, red wax swirls, and
purple dots and strokes.

BASKING IN THE SUN. Sponged background, wax design with
lizard, made with a mold using QuikWood®.

WHAT TIME IS IT? Background is dripped
alcohol inks, plastic lizard colored to
match gourd and Wax Design.

OPAL STAR. Wax Design with textured background, leather strip, and foil feather.

NATIVE BEAUTY. Wax Design, two foil feathers, and leather lacing around the rim. Bead and turquoise embellishments complete the look.

DIAMONDS IN THE SKY. Red background sponged with gold and purple acrylic metallic paint. Wax Design on front, as well as the top of the gourd, is topped off with a sponged foil feather.

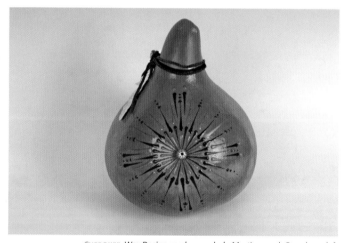

NATIVE PRIDE. Wax Design with textured background, foil feather, and lacing around the rim.

CHEROKEE. Wax Design used on a whole Martin gourd. Gourd was left natural and completed with red and black lacing and foil feather.

MONUMENT VALLEY. Gourd painted to resemble the mittens in Monument Valley. Wax is added to the gourd, making a wonderful sunset.

PAISLEY DOTS. This paisley design was created using just dots. Copper dots were also added.

GRAPE VINES. The branches were painted on. The grapes, leaves, and vines were done in wax. Orange dots were added for an accent color.

DRAMA. The base is blended colors of Radiant Rain. There are twenty-seven different colors of crayon, each leading into the next color. Like our lives.

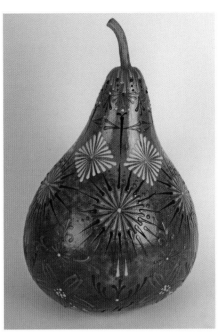

ALL TOGETHER NOW. I started at the top and kept adding designs until I made it to the bottom. This was just a fun gourd to create and share.

SUN WARRIOR. The mask was based with acrylic paint and wax was added to highlight the design.

PURPLE SWIRL. The background is purple alcohol ink. The wax design was added using pink, purple, and silver crayons. Embellishments bring the gourd to life.

SUNFLOWER. The gourd was left natural and the sunflower and leaves were basecoated in acrylic paints. The wax was added to the leaves, sunflower petals, and dots in the center to create the details of the flower.

HAWAIIAN FLOWER. This gourd is colored in silk dyes. Black crayon was used to create the flowers and leaves. The top is beaded.

NAVAJO DESIGN. Start with a natural gourd and divide into rows. The whole gourd is done with one stroke up and one stroke down.

FALL SURPRISE. Wax Design used with leaves made out of QuikWood® and painted with acrylic paint.

HORSE WITH ROSES. Gourd base-coated with black acrylic paint. Design is white crayon with red roses and green leaves.

TURQUOISE DRAGONFLY. The canteen gourd is dyed with purple and turquoise leather dye and then sponged with pearl and gold metallic paints. Wax Design was added. The wings on the dragonfly are actual beetle wings glued on.

FLOWERS. The gourd was dyed with a dark purple ink. The top was cut to accent the flowers. Fine glitter was added to the crayon for sparkle. Pearl accents were glued on.

RED SWIRL. The background is base-coated in black acrylic paint, topped off with a red swirl design.

BRONCO. This gourd is blended with yellow and red leather dye. Horse design is done in black crayon.

FALL LEAVES. The background was created by using alcohol inks. The design was applied using the Wax Design method and the leaves were created out of QuikWood and then painted with acrylic paints.

JUNGLE. The jungle background was basecoated in black acrylic paint. The brilliant green color was a crayon called "inchworm." The other flowers were created using gel Crayolas.

IRIS IN THE SPRING. The oval shape is left natural and sponged with yellow acrylic paint. The outside is purple leather dye sponged with pearl and silver metallic paint. The iris was applied using the wax design method.

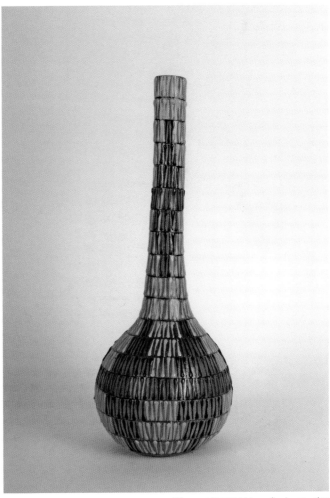

WEDDING BASKET. Using a dipping gourd to create this tall vase, rows were divided off and the wax was applied to create the design.

GRAPE HARVEST. A yellow dye was applied to bring out the natural color of the gourd. The vines were painted with acrylic paint. The grapes were dots of wax, followed by the use of wax to accent the vines and leaves. The top grapes were beaded on one bead at a time.

ROSE PATCH. This gourd was basecoated in black acrylic paint. The Wax Design method was used to create the roses, leaves, and little flowers.

SUPPLIERS

Thank you for purchasing my book, *Miriam Joy's Wax Design Technique*. Regarding the tools and equipment shown or mentioned throughout the book, I have a website at www.miriamjoy.com that features them all, with exception to a few of the products that I do not manufacture.

I use PayPal or any major credit cards for your convenience should you wish to purchase any of the items featured on my website.

Should you wish to contact me, please email me at art@miriamjoy.com. I will make every effort to return your email within two to four days, and if need be I may be able to call you direct. I would love to hear from you!

I can also be reached through several social media online websites such as:

Facebook: Miriam Joy Gourd Creations
Pinterest: Miriam Joy
YouTube: http://www.youtube.com/user/Miriamjoy123

RAW GOURD SUPPLIERS

ARIZONA GOURD COMPANY
Green peeled, cleaned, and cut gourds

ANDREW ANDRIST
167 S. Highway 69
Dewey, Arizona 86327
602-620-2811
928-925-2561

GHOST CREEK GOURDS
Dickie & Linda Martin
www.ghostcreekgourds.com
864-682-5251

GREG LEISER GOURD FARM
Greg & Kathy Leiser
www.gourdfarmer.com
530-735-6677

PUMPKIN HOLLOW
Darrell and Ellen Dalton
www.pumpkinhollow.com
870-598-3568

SMUCKER'S GOURD FARM
317 Springville Road
Kinzers, Pennsylvania 17535
717-354-6118
*no website available

TOM KELLER GOURDS
Tom & Zelda Keller
www.tomkellergourds.com
662-494-3334

WUERTZ GOURD FARM
Waylon & Leah Wuertz
www.wuertzfarm.com
520-723-4432

GOURD TOOLS AND MATERIALS

ARIZONA GOURDS
Bonnie Gibson
www.arizonagourds.com
520-477-7230

BLUE WHALE ARTS
Leah & Berry Reed
www.bluewhalearts.com
603-734-5504

THE CANNING SHOP
Jim Widess
www.caning.com
800-544-3373

GIRAFFES LAFF ART & CRAFTS
Bob & Sherry Briscoe
giraffeslaff@bellsouth.net
336-634-3397

MARIANNE BARNES, AUTHOR
*Weaving on Gourds and New and Different Materials
for Weaving and Coiling*
http://www.maribasket.com